The Perfect Method!

How To Speculate In Stocks In A Bull Trend

BRAD KOTESHWAR

The Perfect Method!
How To Speculate In Stocks In A Bull Trend

Great Expressions Publishing
Scottsdale, AZ 85254

All the characters in this book are fictional. Any resemblance of the characters to anyone living or dead is by accident and purely coincidental. The events in the book may or may not have occurred and may or may not be fictional. If these events have occurred in the past, they might or might not have been used as an example to offer the market's lessons. If the events have not occurred yet, they may or may not occur in the future.

ISBN: 978-1-934295-92-2 (Paperback)

Baseball is ninety percent mental, and the other half is physical.
—Yogi Berra

Stock speculation is ninety percent mental, and the other half is pure luck.
—Brad Koteshwar

Dedicated to:
All the students of the stock market, who never give up learning,
irrespective of the wins and losses, because the learning is never ending.

Stay poised, not too high, not too low.

Table of Contents

Caveat Emptor

This is a book about decision-making. Success in the stock market is about proper decision-making, and decision-making skills do not require a Ph.D. in mathematics, or an advanced degree in accounting. It is all about making the right decision at the right time. Every decision you make must be based on something that you observe, and on what you interpret from your observation. A decision is only a good decision in hind-sight. In real-time, no one knows if the decision to buy or sell a stock is the right one. How then to make a decision in real-time that turns out later to be a great decision? Do you have certain rules that make you place a trade in real-time so that the odds of that being a good decision are very high?

This book is filled with simple price/volume stock charts. If charts are not your thing or if you prefer complicated technical analysis, this book is probably not for you. The stocks and charts and moves covered are all real stocks. However, in an attempt to make a boring topic seem interesting, the charts and stocks are depicted within seven different fictional short stories, each short story using a different real-life stock. It is just by happenstance that all seven stocks are biotechnology stocks. If that is not your thing, then you can pass on this book. There are plenty of books about the stock market to choose from, some even promising big wins just by reading them. Be aware that there are no experts. Only the stock is an expert.

This is a book that covers the basics of successful stock trading operations. The method illustrated in the book works for me. It may or may not work for everybody. You have to find your own edge, your own method if the method covered here is not up your alley. My method keeps me out of lousy market conditions and gets me fully committed to some of the best stocks at the right time. There is no system that works under all market conditions because there are times when one should not be in the market and other times when one should be fully committed in the market.

Some say that market timing does not work. Others say that market timing works but only if you know what to do. Why should one listen to what others say? Had one listened to all the things people have said all your life, would you be where you are today? It is recommended that you undertake the journey on your own and find your own path, instead of listening to others. Just know that the path is not easy. It is hard. It takes time, patience, persistence, and an ability to learn from one's mistakes. And most of all, it requires humility. The stock you are speculating with is always right, it is always smarter, and it knows more about itself than anyone else on the planet. In fact, it even knows about your mental weakness, better than you do. And it will exploit that weakness. That is how smart it is. The excessive research you wish to do matters not one bit. What the stock really knows, it hides from everyone. There is generous amount of publicly available news and data offered as research. The real news is always hidden, no amount of research or predictions or models can dig up the hidden news. Save yourself the pain and stop listening to human beings and their research, and just learn to listen to the stock.

If you do not know how to listen to stocks, then you better start the process of learning. It is a never ending process, but most rewarding when you play the game the right way.

Case Study #1
Learn To Unlearn Everything You Have Learned

Chapter 1:
This Ship Sails Different

The year was 2020. Jacques was a big basketball fan, a real fanatic. His favorite player was Rudy Gobert, a seven-foot professional player from France. Gobert was a member of the NBA (National Basketball Association) team, The Utah Jazz. Being a second-generation son of French immigrants, Jacques was partial to the French and being a tall misunderstood man himself, he felt a kinship with Rudy.

It was March of 2020, as Rudy Gobert wrapped up a media interview after an NBA game when Rudy had suddenly become infamous overnight. Jacques was in the biotechnology business and was well aware of the new corona virus, Covid-19, which was slowly spreading throughout the world. His department had been working for months on a vaccine for the next predicted pandemic. And it looked like that pandemic was here.

That evening after his long day at the laboratory, Jacques was sitting at home having his dinner. In the background the television had the news on in the other room. Jacques and his wife, Marie, were enjoying the paella that Marie had prepared. In between exchanging a few words about the events of each other's day and the occasional sips of wine, Jacques heard the faint words emanating from a television news reporter from the TV in the other room.

"Rudy Gobert, a professional basketball player with the Utah Jazz, was in the hot seat today. After a game, during a media interaction, Rudy Gobert... ..."

Jacques jumped out of his chair and ran into the other room and turned up the volume. He stood there in stunned silence listening to the entire story. Rudy had jokingly reached out and touched all the many microphones in front of him during the post-game media availability a couple of days ago. It had been right after the NBA had issued a social distancing statement as the first news of the Corona virus had been making its way through the entire country. In fact, Rudy had gone out of his way to touch other players and their belongings in the locker room. In Rudy's mind, like in millions of others, it was all just a joke, there was no comprehension of the impending pandemic. No one alive in 2020 had ever faced anything like Covid-19 before.

None of Rudy's actions had gone over well with people who knew the dangers of a virus outbreak. Now, a couple days later, Rudy had tested positive for the virus. Soon enough, some of his teammates tested positive and the entire NBA season was immediately shut down. Just like that, Rudy had become a pariah within the NBA.

Jacques had just stood there staring at the television screen that night. Marie followed him into the room and the two of them stood there in silence. Marie reached out to hold Jacques' hand. He gripped her hand and said, "It is here. This is too fast, well before we are ready. Novavax and Pfizer are still a little behind the eight-ball and we at our lab are not ready yet. This is not good. It is too fast. Just too fast."

"I feel sorry for Rudy. He did not know. He still does not know. Nobody knows just how infectious this virus is. Yes, he was ignorant and therefore, his actions were stupid. But he is not alone. Millions of people are out there not taking this seriously. And we have no solution to stop it or slow its spread at this moment."

Jacques worked for a well-known biotechnology company. His department had been working for months trying to get a vaccine to the market. His boss had come to him months ago and had laid out an elaborate and a strategic plan to develop and market a vaccine for a virus that later came to be known as Covid-19. Corona viruses of various kinds have been around for a long time. It was not until Covid-19, that the common person became aware of corona viruses.

Jacques turned to Marie. "You have to begin social distancing with even more intentionality now. No longer any more get-togethers with your investment club. Try to do everything via group chat. Or a video conference. No more in-person hangouts."

Marie was an avid stock market enthusiast and she and a few of her friends had recently formed an investment club to try and learn all they could about the stock market. She was new to the stock market. It was her Friday night hangout. She used to look forward to her Friday evenings with the investment group, especially since Jacques was tied up with the new project at his lab which kept him at work for long hours.

Marie looked crestfallen. "But, Jacques, that is all I have as my outlet. I cannot be totally isolated without any social contact. You know how much I look forward to my Friday nights with the investment club."

"I know, my dear. But this is really bad. You have no idea how bad it is going to get. It will get worse before it gets better."

The following morning Marie convinced and then arranged for her investment club members to get on a group chat and to suspend the in-person meetings for the foreseeable future. Coming from her, with their knowledge of Jacques' work in biotechnology, they all accepted that in-person meetings were not a good idea. Of the fourteen members of the investment club nine of them joined the group chat. After just one week, to Marie's dismay, one by one all of her investment club members dropped off. She had no one left any more in her investment club. Marie mentioned that to Jacques.

"You know, this group chat thing, it doesn't work. Nothing beats meeting people in person, face to face. My investment club just died."

"I suspected that would happen. We are in a different world now. Give it some time. I think you may have to find a different set of characters. People who are more given to trying new ways with changing times. I will reach out to some people I know, stock market enthusiasts, and let us see if we can get you at least one person with whom you can communicate. Who knows, as time passes you could build it into a bigger club."

The following day Marie called Jamie Blankenship. A name that Jacques had given her with a telephone number. Blankenship was an eccentric older man who had been a stock market operator for decades. He came highly recommended from one of Jacques' colleagues at work. Jacques had handed Marie a piece of paper with Blankenship's name and phone number and there was a short description under the name and number. It was not Jacques' handwriting. It was the writing of Jacques' colleague from his lab. The note said, *"Jamie is a stock wizard, but he is nuts!"*

Jacques said that this Blankenship was a genius about stocks but also very eccentric. According to his colleague at work, Blankenship had made a lot of money in the market and was retired. He still dabbled in the market as a hobby. He was definitely worth a phone call even though he was not very sociable and rather blunt.

Now that the NBA season was shut down, Jacques spent his limited free time working on his vaccine project and pouring over literature about the Spanish flu of the early 20th century. Between his drive to and from the laboratory, most of Jacques' time was spent on his laptop and on the phone with his project members. Marie occasionally caught the conversation between Jacques and his team about something called *mRNA*. None of that made any sense to her. She was getting antsy and decided to call Blankenship.

"Hallo!" barked an old raspy voice on the other end.

"Mr. Blankenship?"

"Yes? Who is calling me?

"I am Marie St. Jean, Mr. Blankenship. How are you? I hope I am not bothering you. I think you know Phil Seitz, who works with my husband at his biotechnology firm. Phil gave us your name. Phil said that you could help me."

"Help you with what?"

"Mr. Blankenship, I used to participate in an investment club that used to meet every weekend before this Covid shutdown. Now everybody just went away, and I am left all by myself to check on the stock market. I am new to stocks. I was hoping you could guide me."

"Can't do that."

"Oh? I am sorry to have bothered you, Mr. Blankenship. I appreciate you taking my phone call."

Marie was disappointed. *Well, that didn't go very well, did it? Why did Phil give us this contact if he was supposed to be nuts? What was the point?*

When Marie told Jacques about the phone call, he felt bad for her. He said he will keep checking with others he knew at the laboratory and see if any other names popped up.

A few days later, Marie's phone rang. Marie answered, "Marie St. Jean."

"Marie St. Jean! I spoke to Phil. He said you were alright. So where do we begin?" It was Blankenship's old raspy curt voice.

Marie was taken aback. She couldn't open her mouth for a moment.

"Are you there, Marie?"

"Yes, Yes, Mr. Blankenship. Sorry, I was not expecting to hear from you. At the very beginning would be great. I am new to this."

"Are you any good at texting? Or Signal or Whatsapp or Telegram?"

"Yes, Mr. Blankenship. I am very comfortable with all of them."

"Just call me *Ship*. I will be in touch. On Fridays, just before the market closes. I have one unbreakable rule, Marie. Only I can initiate the contact. My rule is that you do not contact me. If something actionable happens in the market, I will reach out to you. If you do not hear from me that means you sit still. In silence. It is not going to be easy. Your patience will be tested. Your resolve will be tested. I hope you are up to it. Few are."

Marie acquiesced and was excited. She had not felt this good in a while. Something to look forward to, finally. That Friday, in March of 2020, Marie received the first message from Blankenship on her phone.

SHIP: Hi Marie, what do you know about stock charts?

MARIE: Not much. I don't believe you can predict with charts.

SHIP: Chart attached. What do you *observe*?

Chart 1.1

MARIE: You have marked the volume explosion.

SHIP: What are the prices doing?

MARIE: Price looked to be rising. Until this past week, as this week it fell a lot. First, it rose from a price of $18.23 to $29.61 a share. But this week it fell from $29.61 to $21.30.

SHIP: Your eyes are working fine.

MARIE: What do I do now?

SHIP: Nothing yet. Let's wait and see. I want to see whether it will go under $18.23, the prior low. Or will it go above $29.61, the prior high. Until one or the other happens, you wait and observe it.

MARIE: But won't I miss the move?

SHIP: Maybe. I don't know yet. Let's see what happens next month.

MARIE: Next month? I thought we were messaging every Friday.

SHIP: Watch this stock every Friday, see how it closes the week. Do you have a trading account?

MARIE: Yes, I have an account with an online broker.

Marie was excited. But the excitement died down as she did not hear back from Ship the following week. Another week went by. And another.

10

She was getting anxious and didn't know what to do. *Should I message him? Or should I just sit tight? His unbreakable rule is that I cannot contact him. Is he testing my patience? He did say that my patience and resolve would be tested, so I guess I have to wait it out. I cannot make heads or tails of this stock's chart. It sure seems to be a stock that is rising in price.*

A few weeks later, she finally received a message from Ship.

SHIP: Marie, are you ready to buy?

MARIE: Hi Ship! Nice to hear from you. I thought you forgot about me ☺

SHIP: She was not ready.

MARIE: Who was not ready?

SHIP: The stock. She was not ready. Now she is.

MARIE: Okay! I am so excited. What amount should I buy?

SHIP: What are you willing to lose?

MARIE: Huh? I am buying a stock to make a profit! Not to lose my money! What do you mean by what am I willing to lose? I am *not* willing to lose anything.

SHIP: Then nothing to buy.

MARIE: Wait! I should be willing to lose before I can buy this stock, is that what you are saying?

SHIP: Correctomento!

MARIE: I have to give you an amount that I am willing to lose. Is that what you are saying?

SHIP: Correctomento!

MARIE: But I would be upset if I lost, and Jacques will recommend that I stop this stocks business if I lose money in the market.

SHIP: Ok, bye.

MARIE: Wait, wait, please wait! Let me think for a moment.

A few seconds later, Marie was till silently contemplating.

SHIP: Look at this chart now. The market will close in a few minutes.

Chart 1.2

MARIE: The price is $46.85 a share! It more than doubled from $21.30 last time you showed me the chart?

SHIP: What price is the last low?

MARIE: What does that mean?

SHIP: Look at the V shape. What price is the low point of the *latest* V shape?

MARIE: What V shape? Am I looking at the V formed by $34.84 and $46.85? The low point between those two prices is $31.86. Is that the price you were referring to?

SHIP: Correctomento.

MARIE: What is the importance of that $31.86 price?

SHIP: I don't want her to go below that price.

MARIE: Who is she?

SHIP: This stock. She cannot stop going up.

MARIE: Is she going up in price? How do you know?

SHIP: If she falls below $31.86 then she is telling me that she has no more juice left to keep rising.

MARIE: What do I do if she falls below $31.86?

SHIP: You buy right now. At $46.85. But if she falls below $31.86 you have to sell and take your loss.

MARIE: I don't get it.

SHIP: I know. Most don't.

MARIE: I am scared. It seems like I am throwing my money away.

SHIP: You wanted to learn.

MARIE: Yes, I do. But not by losing 😵

SHIP: You have to be willing to lose to win. You lose to learn; you lose to learn to win. You must lose. That is the nature of the market.

MARIE: Wait a minute. I don't have much time to think. I mean, the market is closing in five minutes for the week. What do I do?

SHIP: Correctomento. No point in thinking. Just do it.

MARIE: How do I figure things out? I don't get the numbers. I am not good at math.

SHIP: Simple. A price below $31.86, let us say we pick $28.67 as the sell-stop. Buy price is $46.85. Potential loss per share is $46.85 - $28.67 = $18.18. This is a small experimental buy.

MARIE: You are going too fast!

SHIP: Place the order. Say you want to test with an amount between $1000 and $1500. I would say 28 shares. Buy at the market.

MARIE: Let me do the math... ... ...Ok. That is $1,311.80. But if it hits the stop I would be losing $500 on this. That is a big amount to lose as a percentage on $1,311.80.

SHIP: It is an experiment. Peanuts.

MARIE: Ok, ok, you are right. Alright, here goes nothing! Done. I bought it.

SHIP: Now enter a stop order. Sell 28 shares at $28.67 STOP GTC.

MARIE: What does it mean?

SHIP: This is a rising stock. My opinion. I could be wrong. If I am wrong, she will fall to $28.67. And she may fall even lower. So, I have decided to sell it at $28.67 right away if she falls to $28.67.

MARIE: What is GTC?

SHIP: You are instructing the broker that the order is good-till-canceled (GTC). So, you do not have to place the same order daily.

MARIE: Why should I make that decision, the decision to sell if it falls to $28.67, today? Why should that decision be made right now? What is the rush?

SHIP: The most you will lose is $500.

MARIE: Yes, but why am I making that decision now?

SHIP: I don't want you to change your mind.

MARIE: I will not change my mind. I already agreed to lose $500.

SHIP: Today you say that. But when your stock drops from $46 to $40 to $35 to $20 and to $18 … trust me, people change their minds all the time hoping it will come back up.

That night Marie told Jacques about her first purchase. Jacques was not paying much attention. He was lost in his own world of lab experiments on the new vaccine his team was working on. And reading up on the experiments and events from the 1918-1920 Spanish flu. Jacques wanted to learn from the previous pandemic.

Jacques heard the words but was not paying any attention as Marie went on and on, "And then I bought 28 shares. I spent about $1,300. I hope you don't mind it. Ship said that at worst, I would not be risking more than $500 on the stock. I know as a percentage $500 out of $1300 seems a lot. But in absolute terms, what is $500? Really, it is nothing in the big scheme of things. I am giving up a couple of dinners out with you now with this social distancing and we have easily saved over $500 in the past couple of weeks. So, I will continue watching this stock now. Ship said to watch for a reaction. It means when a stock rises and reacts to the rise by falling in price. Anyway, I thought… …"

Jacques was nodding but his mind was on his work. On the scientific readings he and his team had been checking that day on their vaccine experiments.

Chapter 2:
The Second Buy

A few weeks rolled by. There was total silence from Ship. Marie was getting used to Ship's sporadic messages and long periods of silence. She remembered that Phil had indicated that Blankenship was nuts. She figured that Phil being Phil was cut and dry about people's personalities. He did not notice the nuances. Marie had found Ship to be very direct and without complications that most humans come with.

Just when she was starting to wonder about Ship, she received a message from him. It was now mid-May 2020. It had been several weeks since his last message and Marie's first buy in the stock market.

SHIP: She is acting well.

MARIE: Hi Ship! How have you been? Hope you are doing ok. Who is acting well?

SHIP: Your stock. She is now at $59.25.

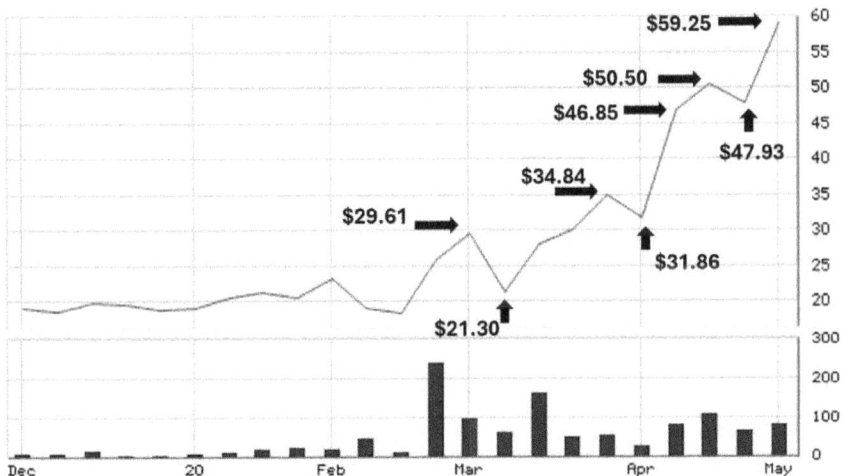

Chart 1.3

MARIE: I am very happy. It has been rising in price.

SHIP: Now what are you willing to lose?

MARIE: What? I am winning. Why would I want to lose?

SHIP: You are happy. She is rising. So, you buy more. So that you can be happier.

MARIE: Oh? I don't know about that. That seems like a bad idea to me.

SHIP: In stocks you execute bad ideas. Because stocks are bad. Really bad.

MARIE: I am nervous.

SHIP: What for? What are you willing to lose now?

MARIE: What do you mean? I already agreed to lose $500. Now I am winning. Why should I want to lose now?

SHIP: Your first experiment worked. Now you have to experiment more. Which means you have to be willing to lose more.

MARIE: What kind of a stock operator are you? This is nuts!

SHIP: The stock is talking to you. She says she will move higher. So, you need to put more money into the stock.

MARIE: Stocks talk to you?

SHIP: If you listen, she will talk to you too. People refuse to listen.

MARIE: I am listening, but I don't hear a thing 😵

SHIP: You paid the stock a fee. The fee you paid was for her to give you a signal. Her signal says that she will go up higher. And for this second signal you have to pay her again.

MARIE: That seems like a scam. She could keep saying that and keep asking me for more and more money.

SHIP: How is that a scam? If you are buying more and more and the price keeps going up and up and your profit keeps going up and up. Where is the scam?

MARIE: She could say that the price is going up and get more money from me and then turn around and go down in price. That would be a scam.

SHIP: So, you tell her that there is a limit to what you are willing to pay as a fee. The first time you told her your fee was going to be $500. That was the amount you were willing to lose.

MARIE: Yes, that is right,

SHIP: This time, initially you thank her for her first message, and then tell her you are willing to lose $1000 as the fee to give to her for her second message.

MARIE: Oh? I have to be willing to lose $1,000 this time. Is that so?

SHIP: She was right the first time. So, you show your appreciation by being willing to pay her $1,000 this time. You know, the first $500 that you were willing to lose, you did not lose.

MARIE: Not yet. But if I am now willing to lose $1000 and I end up losing it, then what?

SHIP: What if you are unwilling to pay $1,000 and she doubled in price? Then what? You missed the move.

MARIE: I did not think of that.

SHIP: If you threw a line and caught a fish, you realize there are fish in the river. And then would you hesitate to throw two lines in the hopes of catching two of them?

MARIE: If you put it that way, then it makes more sense.

SHIP: The first experiment with a small amount worked. See if a second experiment with a bigger amount works just as well.

MARIE: Sigh. All right. What am I looking to do now?

SHIP: The process is the same. Look at the chart. Find the V shape. And find the last low.

Chart 1.4

MARIE: I am looking at the V formed by the prices $50.50 and $59.25. The low between the two prices is $47.93.

SHIP: She should not go below the $47.93 price. Allowing for some volatility, she should not go by more than a few dollars below $47.93. Which means, let us say, the sell-stop is $43.14.

MARIE: What is the buy price? It is now $59.25. Is that the buy price?

SHIP: Correctomento.

MARIE: Does that mean, $59.25 - $43.14 = $16.11 is the loss per each share that I am willing to face if this experiment goes wrong?

SHIP: Correctomento.

MARIE: The most I am willing to lose is $1000. But accounting for the small loss from the previous buy I calculate 55 shares. I buy 55 shares at $59.25 right now. And then place a sell-stop at $43.14. Correct?

SHIP: The sell-stop is on 83 shares that you will now own.

MARIE: Oh, yeah, correct because I have 28 shares from the first experiment and now an additional 55 shares from the second experiment.

That night after dinner Jacques was sitting next to her, reading his lab reports on his vaccine project. She saw a smile on his face. The project must be progressing well because it had been a few weeks of hectic work for him, and he had not smiled in quite a while.

"Is everything ok?" she asked.

"I think we are making progress. It is just frustrating that it is taking longer than I originally thought to get to our milestone. We are there now. We start our next step next week. I am looking forward to it now. After weeks of being nervous about our results, now I see a vague path forward. It does feel good."

"Me too. Blankenship has been great. Outside of stocks, he is tough to be friendly with. But he makes it seem so simple. I am sure it is not that simple. I am making a few dollars, so I am feeling good too."

Jacques looked at her and asked her, "How much are you putting in the market?"

Marie was surprised by his sudden interest in her activity. She picked up a piece of paper, a pencil and her phone and ran some numbers.

28 shares @ $46.85 = $1,311.80

55 shares @ $59.25 = $3,258.75

Total 83 shares = $4,570.55

83 shares at current price of $63 is worth = $5,229

"I have around $5,000 in the market right now."

Jacques nodded and said, "If you are making headway, look to double the commitment. That's what we do in our experiments. If we run a test and it works well, we double or triple our sample size to see if the results can be replicated on a much larger sample size."

Marie was taken aback. She had not realized how Jacques' mind worked until just now. She nodded and made a mental note. Just when she had become more confident, Ship suddenly went silent. It was two months later before she heard from Ship again.

Chapter 3:
The Third Buy

As was typical of Blankenship, he was curt and straight to the point.

SHIP: That stock is still rising.

MARIE: Hi Ship! How have you been? So long since I heard from you! More than two months!

SHIP: Not easy, the waiting.

MARIE: I was talking to Jacques, and he said that if the first experiment worked then I should be willing to increase the sample size and see if the experiment works on a larger sample size.

SHIP: Exactly.

MARIE: Is that why the first experiment was to risk $500 and since the stock went up in price, we were willing to risk $1,000 for the second experiment?

SHIP: Correctomento.

MARIE: The stock is still rising and is now over $90! What now? How much should I look to risk this time?

SHIP: $3,000.

MARIE: How do you know how much to risk?

SHIP: I don't.

MARIE: Then how did you arrive at this $3,000?

SHIP: Instinct.

MARIE: How do I develop instinct? I don't have any instincts about the stock market:(

SHIP: Experience.

MARIE: More waiting, sigh. Ok, now the stock is over $90, so what now?

SHIP: Look at the chart.

Chart 1.5

MARIE: Looks like it will close at $94.85 as we close out this week.

SHIP: Fix the sell-stop.

MARIE: Ok, so the sell-stop will be below the V. But this looks like a W. Between $69.00 and $94.85 it sure looks like a W instead of a V to me.

SHIP: You are smart. Pick the lowest point between the tops of the two sides of the V or W. The lowest point, dear. V or W doesn't matter. Where is the lowest point of the V or the W?

MARIE: Ok, that is $58.19. That means the sell-stop is below $58.19 and I think I would place it at a price of $52.37.

SHIP: Good, good. Now, fix the number of shares you will buy.

MARIE: I don't know how to arrive at the right number ☺

SHIP: Ok, let me see… ….it will be 65 shares @ $94.85. That is the experiment. Can't cut corners.

MARIE: I do not understand this.

SHIP: Rising stock, trending stock. The trend is negated only if the prior low is violated.

MARIE: So, all 148 shares that I now own have a sell-top at $52.37.

SHIP: Exactly.

Later that evening, Marie took out her trading journal. And entered her latest trade positions down.

28 shares @ $46.85 = $1,311.80

55 shares @ $59.25 = $3,258.75

65 shares @ $94.85 = $6,165.25

Total 148 shares cost = $10,735.80

148 shares sell-stop $52.37 = $7,750.76

Worst case scenario if the stop is hit = $10,735.80 - $6,165.25 = $2,985.04 loss

Marie decided to program her mind to accept the loss. She said to herself aloud, "I am resigning myself to lose $2,985.04. I am considering this a fee I am willing to pay to the stock to tell me if I am buying the right stock and if this is the right time to buy this stock."

The following morning at breakfast, she shared her numbers with Jacques and said, "You know, I followed your suggestion. About experimenting with a larger sample size on my stock position. I took a bigger position because my first couple of decisions proved to me that I was doing something right."

"Good for you! I am proud of you. It is a hard thing for most people to do. To take a bigger second risk without knowing for sure if it will pan out. Even though the first smaller risk panned out, when the stakes get bigger the mind starts to doubt. Believe me, I have been there. It is not easy."

Even though Marie was not seeking approval from Jacques, his encouragement gave her confidence.

Chapter 4:
What Next?

Weeks rolled by, which turned into months. There was total silence from Ship. Marie kept a watch on her stock position. From its high of $94.85, a price where she bought her third position, it fell back. When it was $94.85, her account value on her 148 shares was $14,037.80 compared to her cost of $10,735.80. She had a bit over $3,300 profit and she was feeling pretty good about herself.

But the stock market requires one to have a steady balanced approach. Not too high, not too low. When things are good, not to be excited. When things are bad, not to be rattled.

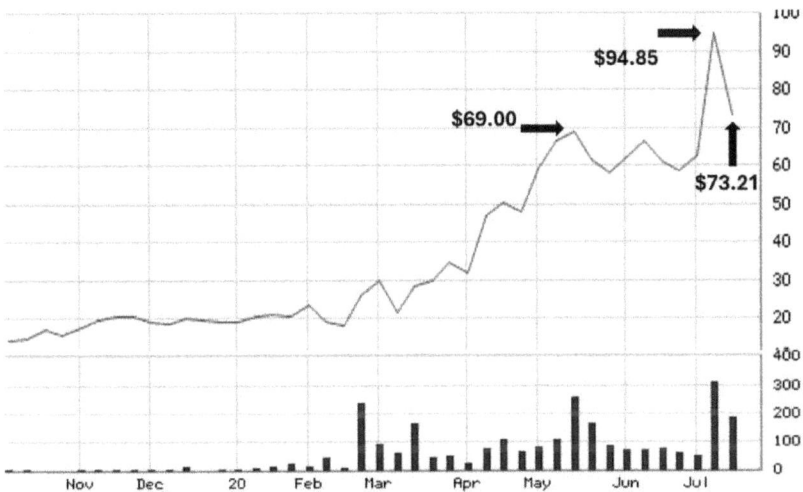

Chart 1.6

Within a week, the stock dropped from $94.85 to $73.21 and her $14,037 was now worth $10,835. All her profits had vanished within a week. She stared at her trading account value on her computer screen, and she couldn't take her eyes off of it.

She had a deep urge to click on sell as she was now scared that the stock would fall further. And she felt that she would end up in the loss column, having given up all her profit. She was biting her lip and thinking. And her phone buzzed.

SHIP: Do *not* do what I think you are thinking of doing!

MARIE: Oh, Ship! So good to hear from you. I lost all my profit in just a week! All these months of torture, anxiety, and poof! Just like that, it is all gone!

SHIP: She will test your resolve. This is the test.

MARIE: Who will test my resolve? The stock?

SHIP: The discipline is to stick to your stop.

MARIE: But I will lose more if she goes lower in price. I have already given up the $3,300 profit I had. Now, I will face losses if it goes lower!

SHIP: Remember, when you placed that trade, you resigned yourself to a loss of $3,000?

MARIE: Yeah! That was then, before I gave up my $3,300 profit.

SHIP: She is testing your resolve. You have to stick to your guns.

MARIE: But I lose $3,000 if it goes down lower and hits my stop-loss price of $52.37.

SHIP: Stay in the present. You are "what iffing."

MARIE: What does that even mean? I have never heard of such a word.

SHIP: What if she goes to $52 and I lose $3,000 when I had $3,300 profit? What if this and what if that?

MARIE: Well, isn't that the way people think about this?

SHIP: Correctomento! You must think the exact opposite! In fact, you should not think about anything at all. Your trades are automatic. No human emotions involved.

MARIE: This sounds so convoluted.

SHIP: This is still at the experimental stage. Let the stock first prove to you whether you are right or wrong.

MARIE: This is lunacy! No wonder Phil said you are a genius but a little bit nuts.

SHIP: Ha ha ha, that Phil, he is a little bit of a nut himself! We all are a bit nuts, aren't we?

MARIE: I am so worried that this stock will continue to drop in price.

SHIP: She can go all the way to $52.38, just one cent above your sell-stop. And still prove to you that she is a big winner. That this is a rising stock and a stock that can make you good money. So, now, sit tight and do not do anything. I will be in touch when the time is right.

The stock's downward draft continued for a few more weeks, with each passing week, Marie got more and more anxious. It went almost to her stop price but not quite. She remembered what Ship had said, that it could go to $52.38, just one cent above her stop and still be a great winner. In September, it had gone all the way down to $59.34 from its high of $94.85. It was just $7 away from her stop.

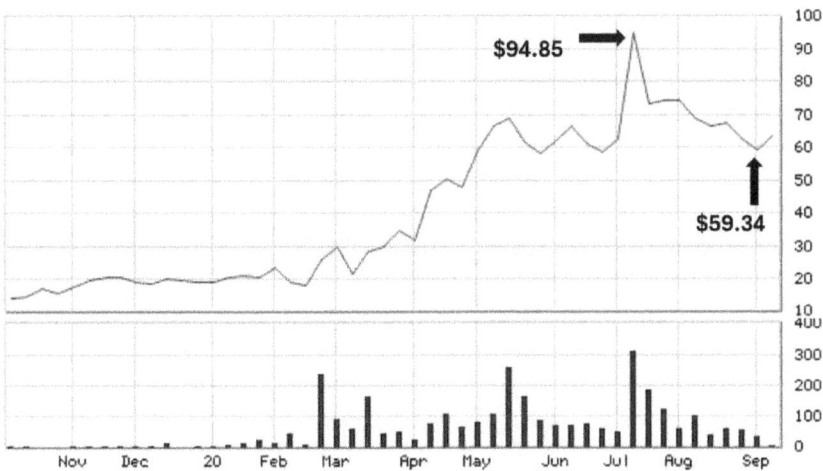

Chart 1.7

She held her breath anxiously as it had dropped from $94.85 to $59.34, and her account value had fallen from $14,037 to $8,782.32. She was now almost $2,000 in the red. She couldn't handle it. Her account value had gone from $3,300 in paper profit to almost $2,000 paper loss. A swing of $5,300! She was beside herself, but she felt trapped by the stock and by what Ship was telling her to do.

Now she was talking to the stock," Come on, come on. Get back up now. Enough with this reaction. That is far enough. Let's get back on our horse and let's start riding again, ok?"

Soon enough the reaction ended, and the stock started its slow climb back up again. The waiting was torturous. Before long, it climbed back up above $80 after having tested prices below $60. After a while, it made a new higher high price. A price above its prior high. Marie could feel it in her gut that Ship would be reaching out. And he did.

SHIP: She made a new high. Still rising.

MARIE: There you are! What's with you and the vanishing acts? Why do you vanish for weeks and weeks?

SHIP: Nothing to do but wait.

MARIE: I notice that you reach out to me only when the stock makes a new higher high.

SHIP: You are sharp!

Chart 1.8

28

MARIE: But it was close to the sell-stop for a couple of weeks. Nerve-wracking. The stock retraced all the way back to $59.34, just barely above the previous low price of $58.19. I was getting nervous, and I thought for sure I was going to lose my $3,000 experimental fee.

SHIP: Stay in the present. No energy to be wasted on something that did not actually happen.

MARIE: I am learning. To think and operate in a more practical way. But when it comes to money, I get nervous.

SHIP: Control the controllables.

MARIE: I am realizing that I need to reprogram my mind. About how it thinks about money. And about decision-making. I need to be more surgical. Clinical. Without thought. Cold. Ruthless in my actions.

SHIP: Bingo!

MARIE: Now what? Do I risk another $3,000? It is too much to risk. I mean, I need to start seeing some profits at some point.

SHIP: Yeah, no more buys until your account breaks even.

MARIE: Oh? My total 148 shares cost is $10,735. That means my average price is $72.53 per share. I have to be able to sell at a price higher than this. Right now, I have a profit since stock's current price is $97.61. Why don't I sell for profit now?

SHIP: Pocket change.

MARIE: Well, now. That may be pocket change for you, but for me it is a profit, Ship.

SHIP: No reason to sell a rising stock.

MARIE: But at some point, it will stop rising. Nobody knows when that will be. Why not bank the profit?

SHIP: A rising stock keeps rising, more and more. Why be in the market for pocket change?

MARIE: You believe that this stock will rise further? How much further? No one can predict.

SHIP: Correctomento.

MARIE: ok, now that answers my question :)

SHIP: My dear, look to buy a huge stake next chance you get.

MARIE: But what if it turns around and heads down in price?

SHIP: Just wait. I will be in touch.

Marie did not understand Blankenship's thinking. She ran some numbers that Friday night. Up until that moment, she had committed a total of $10,735. At the stock's current price of $97.61 she had an unrealized profit of almost $4,000. She had made almost 35% return. *Darn! That is better than most of the money managers, the professionals! Why shouldn't I pocket the profits?*

When Jacques got home and was having dinner with her, she opened a new bottle of his favorite wine. Jacques raised his eyebrows, smiled, and said, "What is the special occasion? Something going on that I know nothing about?"

"I have 35% profit on my stocks, Jacques! But Ship is reluctant to sell. On the contrary, he says to wait for a bit and be ready to place a big stake. I don't get him."

Jacques was calm, took a on his sip of wine. "35%? Wow! That is fantastic, Marie!"

"I know but instead of being happy, I am getting nervous. I will lose what I have if I wait. This is a tough decision to make. "

"I don't know anything about the stock market. But in our lab experiments, when we find that something works, we test it with a large sample size. If it works on a large sample size, we run the test again on a much larger sample size. Then we send it along the chain to get the product to the market. You know, the departments that handle FDA applications, approvals and marketing, advertising, sales, and distribution etc. It is a long process. You have been at this for a short time. From what Phil told me, this Blankenship guy is some kind of a weird eccentric wizard about the market. There is no substitute for experience. I think you should listen to Blankenship. Honestly, 35% on a small investment means nothing. It only means something if it is replicated on a huge investment."

Marie was starting to see the daylight. *Jacques was right. What is $4000 profit? A short vacation for the two of us. It is not a life altering profit. Jacques' approach is the correct approach. Ship does have a lot of experience. Ship has been right so far. Let me wait for some more time and see what happens.*

Chapter 5:
The Right Decision

It had been almost two months since Ship's last message. Somehow the time seemed to have passed faster for Marie. The holiday season had kept her busy. The new year had started, and January 2021 was full of action in the stock market.

SHIP: Are you ready?

MARIE: Happy new year, Ship! Hope you had a nice holiday season. How have you been?

SHIP: Yes, yes. Good. Is the account fully funded?

MARIE: My holiday season was good too, thanks for asking :) What account is funded? I did not get you.

Marie was confused, not knowing what funding Ship was referring to. *Darn! He is so direct, without any human interaction skills!*

SHIP: Your stock trading account.

MARIE: It has enough extra cash sitting in it. I cannot add any more to it. Why? What is going on?

SHIP: It is time to buy. Have you looked at your stock chart lately?

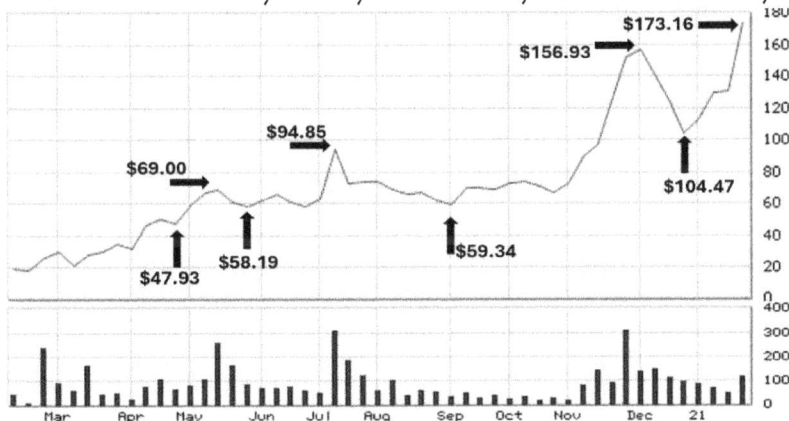

Chart 1.9

MARIE: Yes, I have been watching it. You were right to convince me not to sell back when the stock was under $100 in price. It is getting expensive now. Shouldn't I be thinking about selling now? I have more than doubled my money!

SHIP: Nooo. Buy more!

MARIE: It makes no sense! Zero sense.

SHIP: Do not think with your mind. Observe with your eyes.

MARIE: What am I observing?

SHIP: Every high is higher. Every low is higher.

MARIE: But at some point, it is going to stop rising. No stock rises forever.

SHIP: Stay in the present. Don't predict. You are anticipating and "what iffing" yet again.

MARIE: I am not predicting. I am bad at predicting. That is why I am saying that this stock cannot keep rising forever.

SHIP: It has not gone below its last low. It is rising. You stay in the present. As of today, it has not violated the prior low. No predicting, no anticipating and no "what iffing." Buy today at $173.16.

MARIE: Oh? This is too confusing and so risky. I am so nervous!

SHIP: Why? What is the worst that can happen?

MARIE: I could lose my profit! That is what can happen.

SHIP: Suppose you don't buy today. And the stock is $300 in some months. What would you do?

MARIE: I am sure I will kick myself. But that is not guaranteed that this stock will rise to $300.

SHIP: Nothing is guaranteed.

MARIE: But my profit today is guaranteed. I can sell now and can have doubled my money.

SHIP: What is double your money? Like $15,000 or $16,000 in profit?

MARIE: If I sell 148 shares at $173.16, I will get $25,627.68. I spent $10,735.80. So, about $15,000 in profit! That would be wonderful to pocket it!

SHIP: Peanuts. But you do you. Bye.

MARIE: Wait! Wait! I didn't say I was going to sell and take my profit. I am just thinking aloud.

SHIP: Buy at $173.16. New stop will be $94.02. That is a little below the V tip formed by $104.47 on the chart. $104.47 being the prior low.

MARIE: So how much to buy at this new price?

SHIP: Do not take a loss on a winning stock.

MARIE: What does that mean? The new stop is so far away – at $94.02. The 148 shares I have will only have $94.02 - $72.54 = $21.48 per share profit. That is 148 shares x $21.48 = $3,179.04 – that *is* peanuts! I would have given away so much of my current profit! I would have given up $12,000 out of $15,000 profit and would be left with just a small profit of $3000!

SHIP: Risk all $3,179.04 and do not take a loss on a winning stock.

MARIE: I can only buy 40 shares more at this incredibly high price of $173.16 and not face losses if I get sold out at $94.02. That is not such an interesting proposition.

SHIP: Don't know yet. But play the game the right way.

MARIE: Alright, alright. Sigh. I'll do it.

That night with a lot of apprehension, Marie wrote down her trading action in her journal of secrets.

28 shares @ $46.85 = $1,311.80

55 shares @ $59.25 = $3,258.75

65 shares @ $94.85 = $6,165.25

40 Shares @ $173.16 = $6,926.40

Total 188 shares cost = $17,662.20

Worst case scenario = 188 shares sell-stop $94.02 = $17,675.76

Breakeven! But no loss! I am not sure about this one. I just feel like this is such a wrong move. But I agreed to just blindly follow Ship's direction. Let me see how it goes.

Chapter 6:
More Buys?

It was a few long months for Marie. Her stock kept gyrating. After her latest buy at $173.16 in early 2021, her stock went a little higher to a price of $183.75. And promptly reacted and went down to $132.19. Marie was biting her lip.

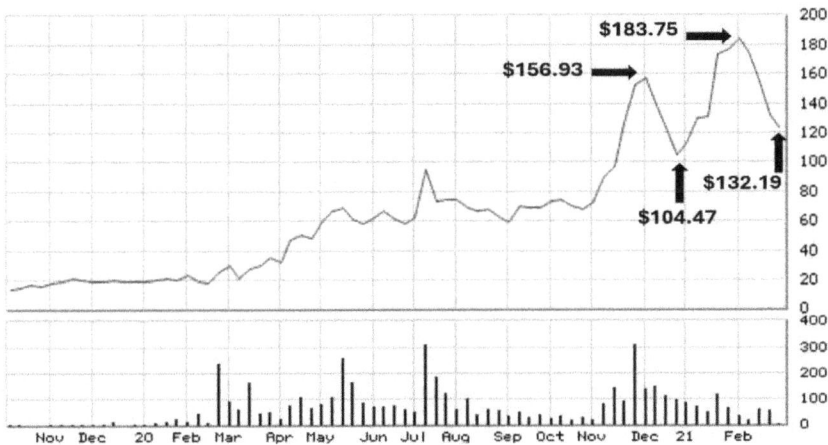

Chart 1.10

Within weeks her stock price had fallen from $183.75 to $132.19, and her account value, which had 188 shares of her stock had fallen from $34,545 to $24,851.72. Her nervousness knew no bounds. She had to control a strong urge to sell. Somehow, she talked herself out of selling. She remembered her earlier experience when the stock had fallen from $94.85 to $59.34 and how Ship had reached out to her just when she was about to throw in the towel.

Chart 1.11

Eventually, in April of 2021, the stock turned up and started moving up and went on to make a new high at $185.01, barely above its prior high of $183.75. But all she got from Ship was a short one-line message that said, "Just wait for a bit more."

The stock continued rising and went on to hit a high at $218.85 before reacting. After logging a high of $218.85, the stock had reacted to $199.19. Yet again, Marie received a one-liner from Ship saying, "Just wait a bit more, hang in there. I will get back to you."

Chart 1.12

In late June 2021, Ship sent Marie a screenshot of the chart shown below. Her stock had managed to make yet another high at $219.94. Marie was giddy. Her 188 shares were now worth $41,348.72. Her cost had been $17,662.20. She had 134% return on investment. She just wanted to cash out her winnings.

Chart 1.13

SHIP: Alright, Marie, are you ready?

MARIE: Yes! I have been waiting for your green light to sell my 188 shares. My seventeen thousand and change is worth over forty thousand now!

SHIP: Look at the chart Marie. The new high is $219.94. The latest low is $199.19. This is the time to swing for the fences!

MARIE: Huh? I am not selling my shares?

SHIP: Where has the stock told you to sell? I have not heard the stock tell me to sell, yet.

MARIE: What am I doing, Ship? If I am not selling, what am I doing? How does a stock tell you to anything, leave alone tell you not to sell! How is that I never hear these messages that you say the stock is telling you.

SHIP: Swing for the fences!

MARIE: I do not understand!

SHIP: All this time you have been buying and your sell-stops have been far away from your buy price. Your profits have been minimal. This is now the first time, and maybe the last time, you will get a chance to buy when the sell-stop is close to the buy price. Moreover, you have a good profit that you can risk.

MARIE: Oh, I don't know about this, Ship. Sounds like a terrible idea. I have been going along with your plan, no matter how outrageously wrong it felt to me. Now, more than ever, this step seems to me to be really a terrible idea!

SHIP: Exactly. In the stock market you do the opposite of what most people would do. If people say doing something is a good idea, then it is a bad idea. And vice versa.

MARIE: I really am very confused by all of this.

SHIP: I am running some numbers. Stay with me. Look at the chart to check what I am suggesting. If you buy at $219.94 and get stopped out at $179.27, a little below the last low of $199.19 your loss per share would be $219.94 - $179.27 = $40.67. That is because $179.27 is a little below the last low of $199.19. In the worst case, your current 188 shares would be worth 188 x $179.27 = $33,702.76. That is a profit of $16,000 on your approx. $17,000 investment.

MARIE: I am really very apprehensive about this. My hands are shaking.

SHIP: Don't think of it as money. Don't pay attention to the account value. Play the game the right way, without paying attention to the score. You will learn to win with time and patience.

MARIE: How can I not think about money as if it is not money? It is money!

SHIP: Think of it as tokens in a casino. Or if you don't go to the casino, just think of the dollars as if they are apples. Ha ha ha...

MARIE: You have a strange sense of humor!

SHIP: Look, suppose you risk $15,000 out of the $16,000 you have in profit. You can buy $15,000/$40.67 = 368 shares. This will cost 368 x $219.94 = $80,937.92. Do you have this in your account?

MARIE: No! Wow! I am not able to put that in stocks as I do not have the money, Ship!

SHIP: Ok, what amount do you have?

MARIE: I have $30,000 more besides what I already put into this stock.

SHIP: Ok, this stock has 30% margin. Your account value at $219.94 is $41,348.72 plus $30,000 cash = $71,348.72. You can easily margin the required amount. Go on margin and buy it. Buy 368 shares at the market now! Before the market closes in the next few minutes.

Marie didn't even have a moment to think and as if in a trance she went ahead and executed the trade.

SHIP: I know this seems counter intuitive right now. Sleep on it over the weekend. See how the market opens on Monday. If you are still nervous go head and unwind the trade. Tell you what, I will reach out to you on Monday.

Somehow, Marie found some solace in that. At least Ship will reach out on Monday, and she will have a chance to reconsider.

On Monday, the stock closed at $222. And Ship messaged her and asked her if she wanted to reconsider. Marie had the time to think it through over the weekend and she and Jacques had come to a decision. They wanted to ride this out. She thanked Ship and told him that she was now willing to stick with the plan, ride out the move, and see where it ends up.

SHIP: Ok, great. Moving forward, I will let you know where and when to move your sell-stop up. This way, if the stock continues to rise, you can move your sell-stop up. I will be in touch.

In July 2021, Ship reached out with a screenshot of the stock's chart, and it looked as shown below.

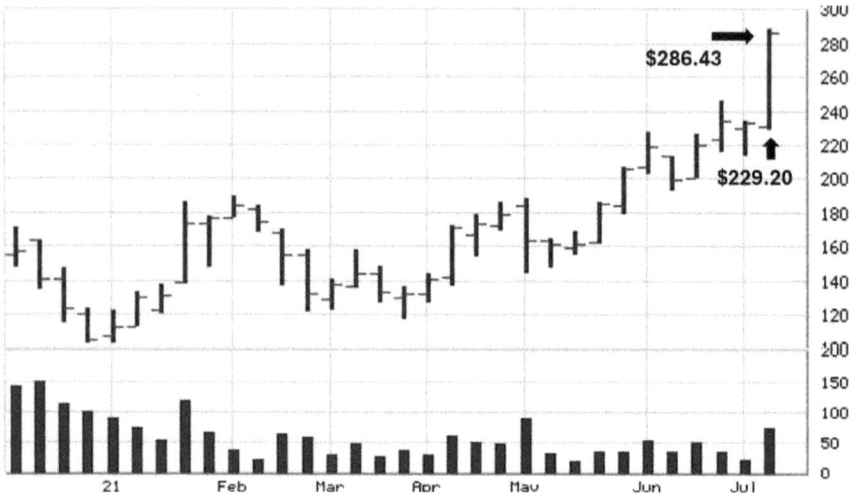

Chart 1.14

SHIP: You can move your stop up now. Say a little below $229.20. Move it to $221. This way, you will now never have the second thoughts you had before. I am going to sign off now.

MARIE: Wait. What?

SHIP: Just keep moving your stop a little below the new weekly low and you should be fine. This stock is making one final push.

MARIE: You are leaving me on my own just when I need you the most?

SHIP: You don't need anybody, least of me.

MARIE: Don't say that!

SHIP: You will do just fine.

Marie took her trading journal out that weekend. And updated her account.

28 shares @ $46.85 = $1,311.80

55 shares @ $59.25 = $3,258.75

65 shares @ $94.85 = $6,165.25

40 Shares @ $173.16 = $6,926.40

368 Shares @ $219.94 = $80,937.92

556 shares total

Total commitment $98,600.12. Margin amount = $50,937.92

Sell-stop at $221.

A few weeks later, in August 2021, she looked at the chart of her stock as her sell-stop got triggered. She had continued to move her stop a little below the latest weekly lows. When the latest weekly low had been $389.78, she had placed her stop $25 below that price at $364.78.

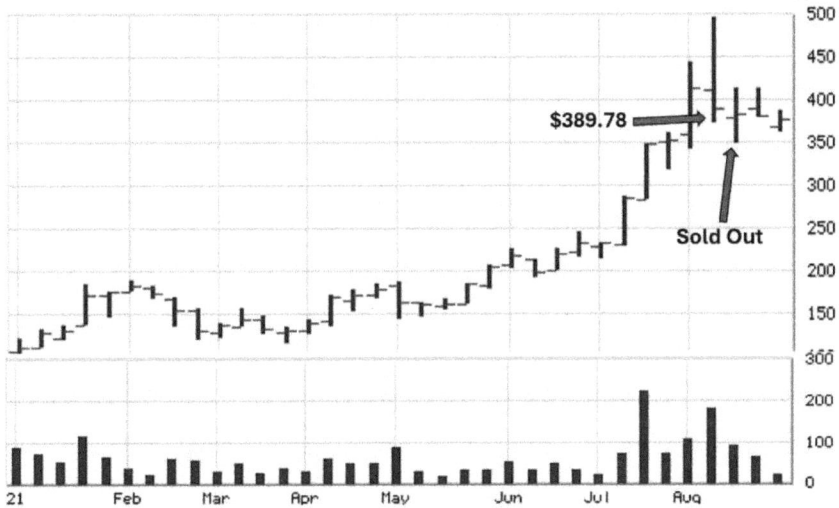

Chart 1.15

That stop was triggered in August 2021. Marie was stunned. She kept staring at her account value and could not believe it. It said her account was worth $202,817.68.

But how? How did this account become so profitable? She had to do the math herself.

556 shares sold at $364.78 = $202,817.68

My out of pocket:

28 shares @ $46.85 = $1,311.80

55 shares @ $59.25 = $3,258.75

65 shares @ $94.85 = $6,165.25

40 Shares @ $173.16 = $6,926.40

368 Shares @ $219.94 =$80,937.92 from $30,000 my funds + $50,937.92 margin funds

My commitment to this operation = $47,662.20

My account value after deducting margin funds returned to the broker =
$202,817.68 - $50,937.92 = $151,879.76

My return = $151,879.76/$47,662.20 = 218%

She couldn't wait for Jacques to come home that evening. She ordered a delivery from her favorite restaurant and had Jacques' favorite wine bottle ready to be opened when he got home. She did not feel like going out. She wanted to just sit down with Jacques and let it all soak in.

She looked at the last chart that Ship had sent her. It was a minute or so before it dawned on her. Her trades in her stock had foretold her what had eventually transpired. Her stock had been Moderna (MRNA).

Moderna had gone on to profit from its approved vaccine for Covid. But her actions, thanks to Ship, had been in advance of the actual reality. Big money had shown its hand just by the way they had helped move Moderna's stock price all the way from Marie's first buy at $46.85 in the summer of 2020, a few months into the Covid experience, to her final sale price of $364.78 in August of 2021.

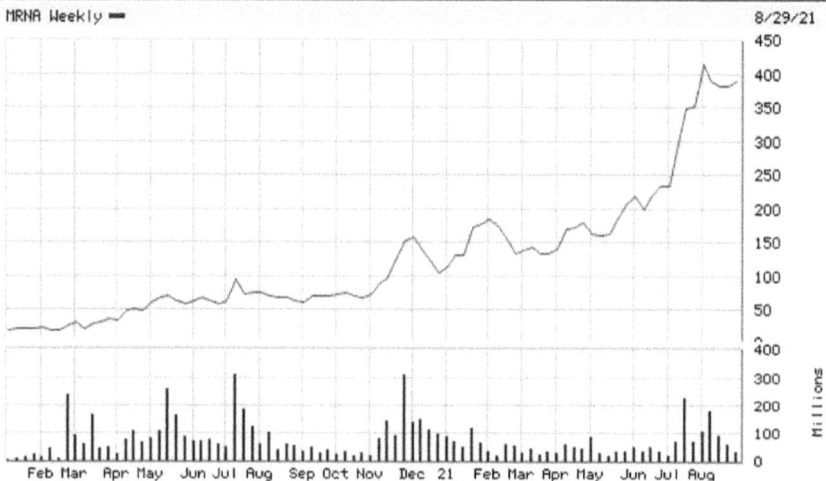

Chart 1.16

44

Jacques' lab had been working with Moderna in their quest to develop a vaccine for Covid-19. Marie was going to let Jacques know that she had somehow known in advance that his work with Moderna was going to prove to be successful. And would pay dividends to the population in general with Moderna's vaccines and also pay dividends for those who played the game the right way with Moderna's stock.

She had capitalized unknowingly on Moderna's stock just by being patient and checking on her activity week by week. *That Ship, he was something. Phil was right about him. Ship's moves had made Marie an insider at Moderna, unwittingly.*

Case Study #2
The Outsiders
Who Act As Insiders

Chapter 1:
The Perfect Pool

Conrad Rhodes was having breakfast at his sister's house that Saturday. It was the autumn of 2018. Cecilia was close to Conrad, about as close as a big sister could be to her little brother. Though they were both in their seventies now, Conrad made it to his Cecilia's every Saturday morning for breakfast. A visit to Cecilia's always felt like home to Conrad.

Conrad was from a generation that read newspapers with their morning coffee. Cecila was jabbering about some strange hand she had to play at a card game, a game of bridge, with her friends the day before. Cecila was an expert bridge player. Conrad was fixated on a chart of a stock in the newspaper. He knew something was up. He had seen the same price and volume behavior many times before.

Conrad placed his folded newspaper slowly on the table. He looked up at Cecilia. She was still going on about her hand at bridge that she had to maneuver the previous evening. Conrad's shrewd eyes narrowed in a smile. He stood up, went around the table, and gave Cecilia a hug and thanked her for a wonderful breakfast and headed out to his car.

Conrad sat in the driver's seat for a moment, silent, without motion. He let the key stay put in the ignition without turning it on. Instead, Conrad pulled out his phone and called David Stonybrooke. A couple of decades back, David's father, Roger Stonybrooke, had been a partner of Conrad's. Conrad and Roger had run a small pool back when it had been quite easy to set up a pool and operate it. These days a pool was referred to with a much fancier name – a hedge fund. The new rules and regulations and the paperwork involved were a bit much for Conrad. Conrad was a throwback, an old-fashioned stock pool operator.

David Stonybrooke had inherited a sizable chunk of Roger's estate. Conrad and David had run a stock operation with each other once before. Conrad had found that David had a lot of the same characteristics and traits as his father. The financial punch that David packed did not hurt either. When Conrad called, David answered right away.

"Good morning, David."

"Hi Conrad! How the heck are you doing? Been a while. What are you up to?"

"Up to no good, as usual. I was thinking. Do you have time for a drink this evening?"

"Absolutely! Where? When?" David sounded almost excited. The stock market had been a dead bird lately. Zero movement. Conrad calling meant there must be something under the radar that was going on in the market.

"Let's meet at Nico's. Will nine o'clock work for you?"

"Perfect, Conrad. Right after the dinner rush and right before the late-night crowd."

Just as David Stonybrooke had figured, Nico's was almost deserted. The last remnants of dinner patrons were heading out. It was too early for the late-night crowd. Conrad was sitting at a corner table, away from any potential human traffic.

Nico's had the right amount of lighting, bright enough to be able to read, yet soft enough to lend the right night-time relaxed vibe. The music was soft. No other sounds were audible. David shook Conrad's hand as he sat down on a chair across from Conrad.

David was much younger than Conrad. Conrad pulled out his phone and showed David a screenshot of a stock chart. Stonybrooke was not much of a stock chart follower. He looked at the chart and then looked at Conrad with raised eyebrows and said, "So? What is going on here?"

"Not sure yet. But something is in the works. I can feel it in my guts. This one's a biotechnology company."

"I am not a big fan of biotechs, Conrad. Too much risk, too volatile. And the last time I was in a biotechnology stock, I got bitten. FDA rejected its drug and within a day, even before I could get out, the stock crashed and burned." David said shaking his head.

"I wouldn't come to you with unreasonably risky ventures, David. That is not me. There is no advantage in my causing us an unreasonable loss with an unreasonable risk. I know how to manage risk."

"I know, I know. It is just an involuntary reaction when I see biotechnology stocks. Too many other pools. Too many players and too many uncertainties."

Conrad ordered a couple of drinks. David was quiet. They were both deep in thought. Their drinks arrived and as Conrad took a sip, he said, "The only problem I have here is it is too early in the process. This one is a young stock. Really young. I usually like stocks which have spent a few more years toiling in the market."

David reached out for Conrad's phone to take a second look at the stock chart. And said, "Alright, Conrad. What do you need? What are we talking about here?"

"Not much. Two million. Each. Between us that would be four million."

David knew Conrad's method. His father, Roger, had been a partner with Conrad on many pool operations. And it was clear to Roger then, and to David now, that Conrad was an honorable man. Everything with Conrad had been fifty-fifty. Their pool would be split fifty percent each in pooled funds. And it would be similarly split fifty percent each in profits. And fifty percent each should there be losses. David nodded.

"How much time?"

Conrad thought for a moment and said, "I don't know but it wouldn't surprise me if the entire operation took as much as two years. It may require us to wait a bit to make our first move."

"All this sounds good, Conrad. But do you even know the details of what this company makes? I mean, I know it is a biotechnology stock. You will be exposed to all the shenanigans that come with it. FDA approval, or FDA rejection. Drug test trials showing lousy results. Or mishandled drug trials. A competitor filing lawsuits. Shareholder lawsuits. Weird judges who make weird rulings on these crazy lawsuits. You know the usual garbage."

"Yeah, I know what you mean. You know that I do not care about all that stuff. Strictly price/volume action. That's all that matters to me. This may not even pan out and we may never get an entry point. I have no way of knowing. It could be that we could have our pool money just sitting and waiting, and waiting, and nothing happens that makes me jump in. We could be back here having a drink and lamenting the lack of action a year or two from today. And we may have to dissolve our idea of our pool without having pooled our funds, with no gain and no loss."

"What? Money just collecting dust?"

Conrad shook his head and said, "We could face a scenario where we have no buys and sells. That is why we don't need to set up the pool just yet. The stock needs to put more time and work before we can commit to it. But when the time arrives, and it is the right time, I wish to know that you would be interested in pooling the funds if I gave you a week's heads up."

Conrad finished his drink. David indicated that he was going to sit back and have another drink. Conrad paid the check and stood up to leave. David asked to see the chart again. Conrad sent the file to David's phone and left.

David Stonybrooke sat there staring at the chart and wondering what it was with charts and Conrad Rhodes. He just had a nose for things. David looked at the stock chart and could not see anything that screamed at him to put together a pool. But from his prior experience with Conrad, he knew he had to be ready to act when the moment was right. He knew he would get a phone call from Conrad at the right time. All Storybrooke had to do was to act quickly and stick to his commitment. Stonybrooke also knew that the phone call may never come. It all depended on how this biotechnology stock acted.

Chart 2.1

They wouldn't know it at that time, but Conrad Rhodes' estimate of two years for the whole game to play itself out was not far from what really transpired.

Stonybrooke had briefly checked into the stock, and he had found that it had issued a secondary offering in May of 2018. The stock had dipped a bit to $45.75 from its prior high price of $61.10. But by the fall of 2018 it seemed to have recovered and had pegged a new high price of $65.20.

Weeks went by, which turned into months. 2018 turned into 2019. Stonybrooke had by now almost forgotten about the stock and his meeting with Rhodes. But the new year seemed to have triggered a thought in his brain and Stonybrooke checked on the stock's chart in early February of 2019.

Chart 2.2

Stonybrooke stared at the chart and shook his head. This stock was not going anywhere. It had gone on to make a lower low at $40.11, below the prior low of $45.75. He figured this was not going the way Conrad had anticipated. And Stonybrooke promptly forgot about Conrad Rhodes and his drinks with him at Nico's.

Almost ten months later, on Monday, 25th November, right before Thanksgiving, as Stonybrooke was heading for a visit to his brother's ranch in Wyoming, he received a call from Conrad Rhodes.

"You thought I had forgotten about you, eh?"

"Conrad! How are you? It feels like ages since we last spoke. What the heck is going on with you these days?"

"Well, about fifteen months ago we shook hands at Nico's on a potential commitment should the right time come about. And..,.."

"Yes, I remember, Conrad. What happened? Last time I checked that biotech stock, a few months ago, it was meandering and was around $40 from what I recall."

"And you thought it was a dud, not going anywhere anytime soon. Well, it has been stirring and looks to be waking up. Just to be prepared in case it does what it looks like it wants to do, I was hoping to catch you before the holidays, and I am glad I got you on the phone. Before you got really busy."

"As a matter fact, I am heading to Wyoming to see my brother. Good timing. A couple of hours from now I would have been out of circulation for a week."

"My lucky day! And yours too. Hopefully. Let's see what happens. But before you leave do you have enough time to make that arrangement for the 2 mill we spoke about?"

"Yeah, no worries. I will have it taken care of. Are you using the same account as our last operation for the pool?"

Conrad replied, "Yes, it is the same account, no changes."

As Stonybrooke hung up the phone and got on his laptop to make the funds transfer, out of curiosity he checked on the biotech stock chart. It seemed to have come back to above the $60 price. But he couldn't notice anything. He just shrugged his shoulders. *That Conrad, he has eyes that see things.*

It was the day after Thanksgiving, a shortened trading day on the exchanges. Conrad Rhodes was planning to go out golfing. He was in Scottsdale, Arizona, which is a golfer's paradise for that time of the year. The weather was beautiful.

Conrad was waiting for the market to close so he could head to the golf course. The biotech he was eyeing for himself and Stonybrooke was acting up that Friday. He wanted to see how it closed out the week, holiday shortened week or not.

As it turned out, the stock wanted to close at $67.43, a new high, and without a thought Rhodes placed his order. He got filled at $67.43. He jotted down his position and his pre-determined sell-stop.

Bought 1000 MYOK @ $67.43 = $67,430

Sell-stop at $57.07

Worst-case scenario loss = ($10,360)

Conrad Rhodes looked at the stock chart one more time. Then he closed his laptop. *Well, after all this time, finally she offered a signal to buy.*

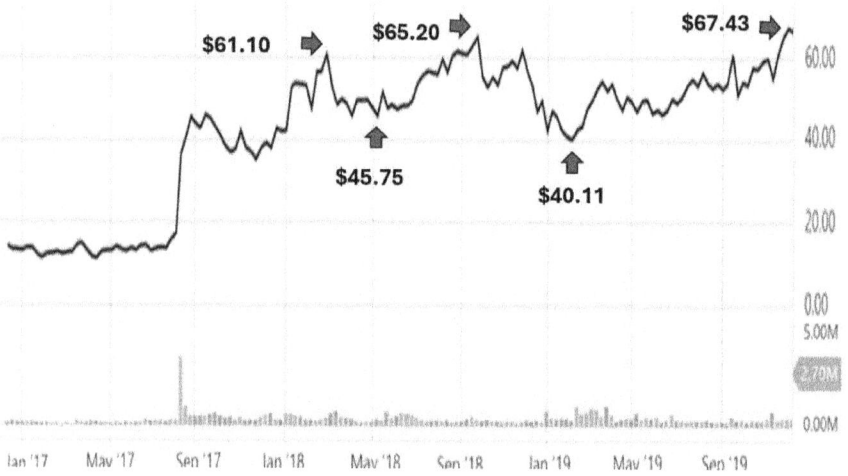

Chart 2.3

Chapter 2:
The Perfect Observer

That weekend went by quite innocuously. On Monday, Rhodes sent a message to Stonybrooke's phone:

Got in on Friday. 67K test-buy. 10K stop-loss.

Conrad knew the message was not necessary; Stonybrooke had given him complete freedom to do as he pleased. But Conrad was an honorable pool operator. One of the very few still around. Conrad had learned from the best, from David Stonybrooke's father, Roger Stonybrooke, who was a classic professional pool operator. He felt the need to keep the younger Stonybrooke in the loop.

The holiday season came and went. The new year, 2020, began quietly. It was an election year. There were beginnings of a murmur of a virus outbreak in China. The people in the know were concerned but the stock market did not seem to be overly perturbed. Until it did get really perturbed in March of 2020, and the market went into a panic mode and a wholesale run began for a few days.

Stonybrooke suspected that the play that Conrad had laid out would be stopped out. And it did get stopped out in early March 2020. Conrad called Stonybrooke.

Chart 2.4

David answered Conrad's call and said, "Hi Conrad. I suppose everything looked good, until it didn't."

"Yes, David. But it still looks good. I have a hunch that all this is just predators preying on the innocent. This will pass and once it does, we may be in for a wild ride."

"This virus thing has blown up the market. I am sure there are opportunities. But it requires some conviction and a lot of discipline I would presume. I know you know what you are doing, Conrad."

"You are right, Stonybrooke. There are going to be incredible opportunities. Let us wait a bit and see."

Conrad Rhodes was not a man with a weak stomach. In his day, he had seen a lot in the stock market. He was biding his time. It didn't take long. Within weeks, in early May 2020, it happened. A breakaway gap and Rhodes knew exactly what to do.

OPEN = $101.91
HIGH = $104.26
LOW = $94.10
CLOSE = $96.90

Chart 2.5

On Monday, May 11, 2020, the stock opened at its all-time high with a gap up on volume. The open price was $101.91. It had closed the prior Friday at $61.09. It had gapped up by slightly over $40 a share. There was excitement for the stock.

But Rhodes waited for the trading day to play itself out. Towards the end of the trading day, the price had drifted down to $96.90. That's when Rhodes pulled the trigger. He jotted down his trade.

Buy 10,000 MYOK at $96.90 = $969,000

Sell-stop at $87.21, worst-case scenario loss = ($96,900)

And he promptly messaged Stonybrooke just to keep him in the loop.

At the end of that week, Conrad opened the chart for MYOK and scanned it for a second. His eyes followed the price and volume action all the way from its IPO to its close on that Friday. As if he was mentally travelling with the stock on its journey from the beginning. He seemed to sense that something was happening, and it was worth being aggressive with the stock. *I should be looking for every opportunity to buy more of this one.*

Chart 2.6

Conrad Rhodes went to bed that night still feeling the inevitable move that he sensed was about to come. He just had to figure out the best way to lay out the pool money, to lay out his line to catch the big fish. His conviction became stronger as he drifted off to sleep.

Chapter 3:
The Perfect Play

That Saturday, Conrad was having his weekly breakfast with his sister, Ceclia. As usual, he was reading the newspaper, sipping his coffee in between bites. And Ceclia was trying to explain the intricacies of her game of bridge from the night before. It all felt very familiar, and Conrad appreciated the regularity, the routine, the simplicity, and the sureness of these Saturday mornings with Cecilia. It was the stability he could rely on, the exact opposite of his experiences in the stock market. Cecilia grounded him as she had all his life.

The years Conrad Rhodes had spent trying to learn the way to be successful in the stock market had been long and challenging. He and Cecilia had grown up in a lower middle-class family and through years of hard work, learning the discipline of persistence from his older sister, Cecilia, a corporate finance lawyer, he had crafted out a very successful stock market journey. Whenever his successful forays got to his head, he would be brought down to reality, to earth by the steadiness of Cecilia.

Conrad needed that. The wild successes he had experienced could have made most humans believe they were invincible. The fall of many a successful trader is the mind, the ego, the lack of humility and the rush of a big win that makes one feel like they could do nothing wrong. And lo and behold, the very next trade wipes them out.

Cecilia kept Conrad real, simple, and true. A man of few words when it came to personal feelings, Conrad would always show up and through his physical presence try to reciprocate the steadiness offered by Ceclia.

As he stepped out and got into his car, Conrad sat and looked at himself in the rear-view mirror. He gathered himself and knew that the next move that was coming with his stock would require him to set aside all human feelings and do the exact opposite of what a typical human mind would do. He drove away from Cecilia's home, leaving behind all human emotions and feelings where they belonged, at Cecilia's home.

Rhodes knew well that there was no room for human tendencies in the stock market. He considered himself lucky to have Cecilia in his life. All human tendencies he had could be used up at her house and when he went back into his pool operator's life he was unencumbered. He could operate with cool confidence, total aloofness, and complete detachment.

Summer was in full swing. It was late July with August just around the corner. Rhodes had just returned from a vacation. His mind was fresh. He believed strongly in maintaining his own counsel with himself. It was a Friday, a few minutes before the market closed. He was looking at himself in the mirror, and the need to talk to himself arose. About his pool operation. His stock had retreated from its last high price of $121.69. And was slowly approaching his sell-stop price. He recalled his last trade entry in his book of trade secrets.

Buy 10,000 MYOK at $96.90 = $969,000

Sell-stop at $87.21, worst-case scenario loss = ($96,900)

Conrad spoke to Rhodes who was staring back at him in the mirror. "You are less than $3 from your stop. Less than 5% away. This retraction is a buying opportunity. What is the worst that can happen? On already accepted $96,000 loss, what is a few thousand dollars more of risk? Nothing. Why don't you get a bit aggressive and test if the stock really has the conviction and strength to make new highs."

He calmly walked to his laptop. And placed a trade. And he wrote down his position in his book of trade secrets.

Buy 20,000 MYOK @ Market.

Filled at $90.13.

Total commitment:

10,000 MYOK @ $96.90 = $969,000

20,000 MYOK @ $90.13 = $1,802,600

30,000 MYOK Stop @ $87.21 = ($2,616,300)

Worst-case scenario loss = $969,000 + $1,802,600 - $2,616,300 =
($155,300)

In his mind he did a rough calculation, and his risk exposure was less than 6% of the total amount committed. *Peanuts.*

Before he closed his laptop, he looked at the chart as the week came to an end.

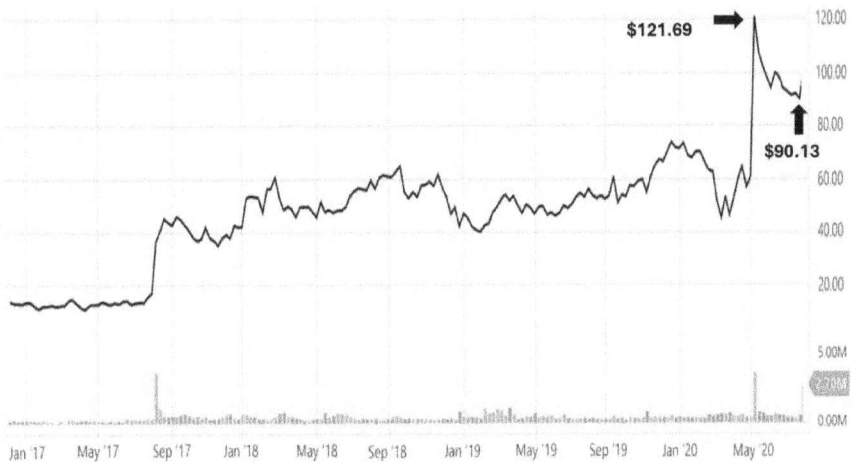

Chart 2.7

The following week, MYOK was back on its feet again and started moving higher. Rhodes didn't care. His operation was methodical, not based on prediction, but on reaction to what the stock did in real-time. He had already been mentally prepared to face a loss of $155,300. He had taken his turn, and now it was MYOK's turn to make a move.

Conrad did not have to wait long. By late August, just prior to the Labor Day weekend, he was presented with an opportunity to make his next move. MYOK had finished making its move, and Rhodes had to make an immediate move in reaction to MYOK's move. The chart was speaking to him. The speculator's mind was now in sync with the stock. It was like a dance, both in sync with each other. Conrad's eyes observed the stock's move and reacted to it. The stock in turn made its next move, and Conrad reacted again.

Chart 2.8

MYOK recovered from its most recent low price of $90.13. And had gone on to peg an intermediate high at $103.40. Conrad sat tight. There was not enough of a clue to do anything. MYOK placed a reaction low to the intermediate high of $103.40 at $99.24. There still was nothing for Rhodes to do. But in his bones, he could feel a move coming. He had to be ready to spend what he could from his pool. He waited.

It was two weeks later that the time came, the time that Conrad was waiting for. MYOK pegged a higher high to the $103.40 intermediate high. MYOK seemed to want to close the week at $103.83. And Conrad pulled the trigger.

Buy 11,830 MYOK @ $103.83 = $1,228,308.90

All pool funds committed:

10,000 MYOK @ $96.90 = $969,000

20,000 MYOK @ $90.13 = $1,802,600

11,830 MYOK @ $103.83 = $1,228,308.90

Total 41,830 MYOK, funds used $3,999,908.90

New Sell-stop $95, worst case scenario 41,830 x $95 = $3,973,850

I would face a small loss of ($3,999,908.90 - $3,973,850) = ($26,058.90)

Now he was fully committed, and in the worst case, he would have a minimal loss, and a small pocket change, less than 1% of the total funds. It felt right. He sent a message to David Stonybrooke, "We are all in now, worst-case less than 1% loss!"

A few weeks later. MYOK pegged a brand new high at $136.56. Conrad thought about the next move. He was out of funds. He looked up the margin requirements for MYOK and was not encouraged as the stock had a special 100% margin requirement. Which meant he had to talk to Stonybrooke about his thoughts. He would have preferred to keep his thoughts and actions to himself, despite Stonybrooke being an equal partner in funding the pool he was operating. With no choice but to reach out to David Stonybrooke, Conrad called him.

Chart 2.9

David answered the call, "Hi Conrad. How are you?"

"It is all going great, my friend. I am faced with a situation that requires us to have a chat. I wonder if you have a few minutes for me this weekend."

David suggested, "Let's get back to Nico's. Last time it offered plenty of privacy. Nine o'clock tonight."

Without thinking, Conrad made his way back to the same table at Nico's where he had met with David Stonybrooke when he had made the original arrangement of funding the pool. He was a few minutes early and decided to order a couple of drinks for the two of them while he waited. Stonybrooke also walked in a few minutes early and joined Conrad, pleasantly surprised that his drink was waiting for him.

After a brief handshake, Conrad got down straight to business and laid down a chart for MYOK on the table. He pointed at the week's close and the week's low price and said, "I wanted to make another purchase today, but this stock is not marginable. So, I missed the opportunity. However, I am hoping it will give us one more last chance to buy but I didn't know how receptive you are to adding to the pool."

Stonybrooke looked at the chart. It didn't make any sense to him. His eyes moved up from the chart to Conrad. "I am committed to a lot of ventures right now. I am not sure what I can shake loose."

Conrad responded, "I will be honest with you. I am going to proceed with this next phase, assuming an opportunity presents itself. It may not even happen, but if it does happen I would like to jump on it. Since the pool has your funds, I wanted to let you know. I will make a move on my own account. But if you wanted to add to the pool, I would match the amount in the pool instead. Then there would be no need for me to make my move separately."

David said, "I appreciate that, really, Conrad. It was not necessary to let me know. You are very honorable; they don't make folks like you anymore. I am honestly tied up to the hilt. I wish I could jump in on this. By all means, do what you want to, there is no need to let me know. You have no idea how appreciative I am. I wish I could join in."

Now having a clear conscience, Conrad waited for MYOK to make its next move. Again, it didn't take long. Two weeks. That's all it took. The first week was a reaction to the high placed at $136.56. The reaction low was $132.72. The following week, on Friday, it seemed as though MYOK wanted to close at $139.60. That was the sign. The sign Rhodes was waiting for. And he placed his trade.

Buy 10,000 MYOK @ $139.60

Sell stop at $130. Worst case scenario loss = ($96,000)

But I already have a profit to cover this loss from my pool operation

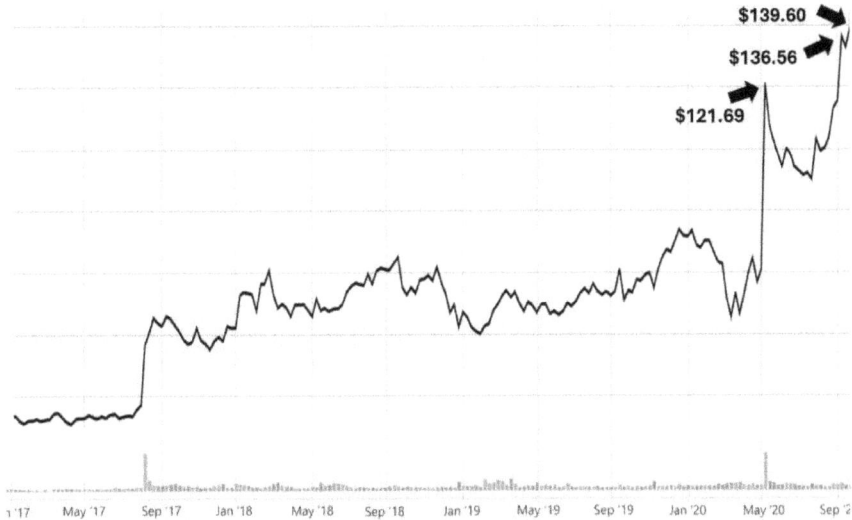

Chart 2.10

The stock closed that Friday at $139.60. The following Monday, Conrad woke up, had a cup of coffee, and headed to his laptop. He turned it on, and it was just a few minutes before the market opened. He clicked on his premarket trading screen to check on pre-open prices. And he blinked. He was not sure he was looking at the correct ticker.

So, he typed in "MYOK" again to check on the pre-open market price. His eyes opened wider. He sighed and smiled and closed his laptop. Slowly walking to the window overlooking the valley below, he took a slow sip of his coffee again. The game had ended. MYOK had gapped up at $224. The play and the operation came to an end. MYOK was bought by Bristol Myers Squibb at $224/share. Unwittingly and without knowing in advance, Conrad Rhodes' pool operation had made him and David Stonybrooke insiders to the entire buyout operation. They were on the outside, with no knowledge of the impending takeover of MYOK. There were the outsiders who acted like the insiders by simply using the stock's price/volume action.

Chart 2.11

The 41,830 shares of Myokardia in the pool were now worth over nine million dollars, the initial pool was funded with four million dollars. Conrad had more than doubled the pool. Separately, Rhodes had made $850,000 in his private trading account. All in all, Rhodes walked away from it all quite satisfied with the operation.

Stonybrooke called Conrad. "Very nicely done, Rhodes! Regret not being able to jump in on that last week's action. Perils of being in real estate. No fast access to liquidity. Too bad that Myokardia stock was not marginable."

That Saturday Conrad spent a little more time with Ceclia, he wanted to feel at home a bit longer. The world of stock operations was far away from his mind.

The following morning Stonybrooke opened his weekly issue of Barron's. It was a small column hidden somewhere in the middle of the issue. He had to scan his eyes through several pages to find it. Buried among a sea of financial news was a column briefly offering news about Bristol Myers Squibb's acquisition of Myokardia. To Stonybrooke's eyes it was just a bunch of baloney, not much of an interesting read.

Bristol Myers Squibb To Acquire Myokardia for $13.12 billion In Cash

Blah blah blah ... ... Myokardia's Mavacamten is a potential gamechanger in treating cardiomyopathy ... ..blah blah blah ...

Somehow after the trouble he took to locate the article, David Stonybrooke's eyes glazed over the details of the story. It did not seem to matter anymore. The story had ended well for him and the aftermath did not matter to him. He folded the paper and slapped his table with it and stood up smiling and shaking his head. *Damn! That Conrad Rhodes was something!*

It was sometime later while reading another column about mergers and acquisitions in the biotech sector, he noticed a short comment from someone named Renata Wierink. He read her comment. It read:

The Behind-The-Scenes Report - The Myokardia Bonanza

Myokardia was an unknown biotechnology company a few years ago. Like any young biotech, Myokardia went through early rounds of financing on the promise of a newly developed drug. In Myokardia's case, the drug was called Mavacamten, a drug to help patients with cardiomyopathy. Cardiomyopathy is a heart disease that makes it hard for the heart to function properly.

After the usual time and financing options had passed, Myokardia went public with its IPO in 2015. Originally, it had a loose arrangement and partnership with Sanofi. Call it an engagement in the hopes of it leading to a marriage. But as time passed, the engagement felt unfulfilled from Myokardia's perspective. There seemed to be a lack of full commitment with both minds not being on the same page. Quite common when human beings are involved, quite similar to a couple who are engaged to marry but somehow with passage of time it falls apart. One party feels like the other party is not equally committed to the same goals and disagrees on the right path to the goals.

Sometimes it is better that the dissolution occurs earlier rather than later. In the case of Myokardia and Sanofi that seemed to the case. Along the way, after its IPO in 2015, and with some more passage of time and drug trial results and FDA approval etc., the stock price of Myokardia reflected the ups and downs at each juncture. Though the timing could not be pinpointed by most investors. Somehow the move always seemed to happen well before the news came out.

There were a couple different times when Myokardia offered a secondary and even a tertiary public offering of additional shares on the market. Myokardia's additional public offerings seemed to coincide every time the share prices of Myokardia had made some progress. Clearly, the handlers pushed the prices up, only to capitalize on rising prices by issuing more stock.

After a while, Myokardia gapped up to above $100 a share, for the first time crossing the $100 price mark. It had closed the prior Friday at around $60 a share. Something was afoot. There clearly was a set of insiders who knew what was in the offing as the share price of Myokardia jumped suddenly by $40 a share.

After a few weeks of consolidation, Myokardia's stock jumped to above $130. And not so shockingly, news came out suddenly that Bristol Myers Squibb had acquired Myokardia for a cash deal valued at 13.1 billion dollars or a price of $224/share of Myokardia. Shares of Myokardia had closed at $139.60 on the Friday prior to the news of the acquisition of Myokardia by Bristol Myers Squibb. And the following Monday, Myokardia was at $224/share. It must have been some weekend. A bonanza for the people in the know!

Case Study #3
You Have To Be Blind To Observe

Chapter 1:
Seeing Versus Observing

Sonia was in her sixties. She looked a lot younger. Some years back she and her husband were involved with a pool operator named Roger Stony-brooke. After Roger had retired and eventually passed away, Sonia and her husband were managing their own trading account. Then the years went by, and Sonia was now alone after she lost her husband in a car accident. The same accident also left Sonia blind.

For the most part, Sonia had acclimated quite well to her new reality. She was now great with her walking cane. Her service dog also helped her out a lot. The one area that she could not function any more was in observing stock charts. The loss of sight hit her the hardest when it came to studying stock charts.

With the help of her son, Sonia had poked around in her social circle looking for someone young who could assist her in studying charts. One day, out of the blue she received a phone call from a young woman.

"Good morning, Sonia. I am Renata Wierink. I was told by Ms. Cecilia Rhodes that you were looking for someone who could help you with stock charts. Are you still looking for someone?"

"Hi Renata. Nice to meet you. What a Dutch name!"

"Yes, my father is Dutch, but I grew up here in Arizona. You know much about Holland?"

"Yes, in fact, I spent two years in The Netherlands as a young woman, in music school in Amsterdam. But that was a lifetime ago. I am so thankful you reached out to me. Yes, indeed, I am looking for an assistant to help with charts. I am now blind due to a car accident, and I miss being able to study stock charts. Are you familiar with stock charts?"

"I am sorry, Sonia. I have no clue about stocks or charts. But I can learn. I am a quick study."

"You know Cecilia Rhodes? You sound so young to know her. I mean Cecilia is way older than you. I can't imagine you and her in the same social circles."

"Yes, Sonia, Ms. Rhodes is my mom's bridge partner. They play bridge every week. My mom asked me if I would be able to assist a friend of Cecilia's. I find Ms. Rhodes to be quite hilarious, a very sharp wit with an equally sharp mind."

"Yes, that she is, ha ha ha, really sharp that one. What do you do, Renata?"

"I just graduated from New York University with a degree in journalism. I will start working for a private investors group as an information digger in six weeks."

"Well, now, Renata! Congratulations on the degree. But I have ever heard of an *information digger*. What does an information digger do?"

"Ha ha ha, to most people I usually refer to myself as an investigative journalist. But I figured you would probably appreciate the term."

"You are funny. I feel comfortable with you, Renata. If you are available and willing, I would like to hire you. I need just one hour every Friday afternoon. If Friday afternoon is not possible, any time during the weekend works just as well."

After a few more minutes spent on the phone call finalizing the fee for Renata's service, Sonia hung up and breathed a sigh of relief. *Finally, some help in overcoming this loss of ability to observe stock charts. It couldn't have come at a better time. I have now found my eyes to observe stocks! A couple of these biotechnology stocks were primed for a move before the accident. Now I can observe, interpret, and act.*

That Friday Renata arrived at Sonia's house. After a brief exchange of niceties, the two of them sat down across from each other at Sonia's breakfast table. It was December 13, 2019. Sonia asked Renata to open her laptop and go to Yahoo Finance website. And Sonia placed the latest issue of Barron's weekly next to Renata and instructed her to look at the charts on Yahoo Finance of all the stocks that were shown as making a new 52-week high price for that week in Barron's. There were quite a few of them.

It took the better part of two hours before they had gone through the entire list of stocks making new 52-week highs. For each stock, Sonia instructed Renata to go to Yahoo Finance website and insert the ticker symbol of the stock and pull up its price/volume chart.

"Here is what I am looking for. Any stock that has made a new high with an accompanying volume explosion is of interest. When you see an incredible jump in the height of the green volume bar in the x-axis, we stop for a second and you have to give me more information. When we come to such a stock, with the right kind of price/volume action, I will let you know what I am looking for."

Renata went through the charts of new 52-week-high stocks, one by one, methodically. At first it seemed a bit confusing to her. Until she came to a stock called Forty-Seven, Inc. Ticker symbol FTSV. When Renata saw that its volume had jumped significantly along with its price for the week, she brought it to Sonia's attention.

"Here is one that seemed to have jumped a lot in price this week. Here it says that this week FTSV went from $14.44 to $35.75. Oh, wow! That is really a lot of price increase! I wonder why?"

Sonia sat up straighter. She seemed to sense the excitement in Renata's voice, but more importantly, she felt the familiar feeling in her own gut. Something surely happened to FTSV.

"Renata, please look at its volume bars, the green bars on the x-axis. Did the volume also jump from last week to this week?"

Renata checked and compared the volume of trade of FTSV and exclaimed, "Oh, yeah! The volume jumped as well! By a lot! By more than ten times!"

"Do you know when this stock's IPO occurred? I mean when does the chart start for FTSV on your Yahoo Finance chart if you select *Max* for the time frame?"

Renata was confused. She couldn't comprehend. So, Sonia tried to make it easier for both of them and suggested, "Could you do me a favor. Could you please take my index finger and use it to trace the price line for FTSV for the past twelve months?"

Renata held Sonia's right index finger and traced it along the price line on her laptop screen, from left to right. She felt Sonia's back straighten up when Renata moved Sonia's finger along that Friday's price and volume jump. The almost vertical move up after a long slow horizontal move was unmistakable.

Renata heard Sonia mutter the price under her breath, "$35.75, that is new high close, $35.75."

Chart 3.1

Renata did not know but Sonia was able to picture the chart of Forty-Seven Inc. (FTSV) in her mind's eye. Years of dealing with stock charts had programmed her mind in a certain way. She could smell a winner. And Forty-Seven was smelling like a potential winner to her. She had an instinct, despite her lack of sight, the instinct was still there. Sonia smiled to herself.

Chapter 2:
Interpreting The Observation

That night, Sonia lay in bed, unable to sleep. She kept replaying the price move of Forty-Seven, Inc (FTSV) in her head. Something has happened. Obviously, nobody on the outside knows, but the insiders definitely know what it is that happened. It serves the insiders no purpose in letting the outside world know what happened. They want to keep it quiet and discreet.

I need to get in on the act. But if I am wrong or if this is a game being played by one heavy-hitter and the stock turns around and heads down in price, I need to have a fail-safe, a stop price at which I am sold out to protect my trading capital. This week's action surely warrants me getting in, but without a proper stop price, I have a hard time committing. I need to watch this stock for a better entry point.

Renata kept to her schedule and arrived on time for the following Friday's charts work with Sonia. There were many stocks that seemed interesting to Sonia. However, she was fixed on Forty-Seven, Inc. (FTSV) for some reason. For two weeks in a row, Forty-Seven Inc. (FTSV) kept rising. From a close on the first week at $35.75 to $40.88 the following week, to $44.05 the week after.

Chart 3.2

79

Sonia was now even more convinced that something was happening. Could be anything. Maybe they have a pending FDA approval for their drug in the pipeline that seems promising or could be some of their drug trials are showing positive results. Or maybe their R&D has found something that needs an infusion of cash, and maybe that is leading to insiders running up the price so they can issue a secondary stock offering. Thus, raising cash for their operations.

Or there is someone big, a big pharma looking to buy up Forty-Seven, Inc. (FTSV). That takes weeks and months and may even take over a year. And in the end, after all the negotiations, it may fall apart, and the stock price could come right back down.

Too many uncertainties. But there was clearly something unusual happening and Sonia wanted to get in on the stock price rise, but she was not clear where to place her sell-stop to get out in case she was wrong. So, she waited.

For the next couple of weeks, the stock reacted and headed back down. It pegged a low of $35.28. It was now the new year, 2020. Sonia could feel a sense of conviction within her. She asked Renata if you could come earlier on Fridays.

Chart 3.3

"How much earlier would you like for me to come by?"

"Well, the market closes at 4:00 pm. I would like you to come at least thirty minutes before the market closes. Will 3:30 pm work for you?"

"Sure, that is no problem at all, Sonia."

The following Friday was quite eventful for Renata. It was her first experience in seeing how a stock trade was placed on the phone. It was strange because she had seen in the movies and on television shows that people placed their trades online.

Renata arrived at 3:30 pm at Sonia's house. Sonia had asked Renata to open her laptop and open Marketwatch.com. And Renata was instructed to enter the ticker symbol FTSV on Marketwatch.com. It said the price for FTSV was $46 per share. Sonia asked Renata to leave the screen on. The market was still open for another thirty minutes. Sonia made coffee and offered Renata a cup. There was silence for a few minutes. Renata felt a need to fill the silence. Renata noticed the price for FTSV was moving up and down between $46 and $46.50.

"This is nice coffee. I usually do not drink coffee this late in the day, but this feels so fresh."

"I suppose you are wondering what we are doing having a cup of coffee instead of working on the stock charts. I need to wait till the last 15 minutes before the market close and check where Forty-Seven seems to want to close for the week. We have a few minutes to kill. What price is your screen saying Forty-Seven is selling at?"

Renata looked at her screen and said, "$46.70, and we have another twenty minutes or so before market close."

A few minutes later, Sonia picked up her phone and called someone. Renata sat there listening and wondering who Sonia was calling.

To Renata it seemed like Sonia punched some codes in on her phone and she was then talking to a human voice, a male voice. Renata could hear the voice of a man on the other end of the call ask Sonia to authenticate her identity via a couple of questions. And then Sonia said, "I want to place an order."

"Ok, go ahead, Ma'am"

"Buy 1000 FTSV at the market."

"One second please … … ..ok, you are filled at $45.74, Ma'am."

"I would like to place a sell-stop. Sell 1000 FTSV at $31.75 Stop GTC."

"Ok, one moment please … … ok, your stop has been placed, Ma'am."

Sonia thanked the man on the phone and placed her phone down.

Renata and Sonia then finished their coffee in silence.

"What just happened?"

Chart 3.4

"Oh, Renata, I just bought a thousand shares of Forty-Seven. I have a feeling this stock will go up in price. We will see. Just have to wait and see. Could you do me a favor, and write down these numbers in the small notebook on the table?"

Renata scanned the table and saw a small nondescript looking notebook near the middle of the table that had a pen next to it. The little notebook had a sticker on the front cover with a pretty feminine handwriting that said, "*Journal Of Trade Secrets.*" Renata picked up the notebook and the pen and opened it. The first several pages had notes with prices and what looked like stock sticker symbols.

"You can skip the first few pages that have my prior trading records and find the first blank page."

Renata flipped the pages until she came to the first blank page and looked up at Sonia and said, "I am ready."

Sonia asked Renata to write down her trade details:

Bought *1000 FTSV @ $45.74*

Total committed = $45,740

Stop price $31.75, worst-case scenario loss = $45,740 - $31,750 = $13,990

Renata kept a straight face, without showing any reaction, she jotted down the trading record. As she walked out of Sonia's house, Renata thought to herself, *Wow, she is risking forty-five thousand dollars based on just my verbal price details of a stock chart! Maybe she researched the company in her own time. But how? She cannot see, so she cannot read. Does she have someone reading to her? Astoundingly courageous, my goodness.*

Renata had no way of knowing but Sonia's exposure to risk was no more than fourteen thousand dollars. Renata was still young and inexperienced to understand that if you know what you are doing, you do not look at risk the same way as most others do.

Chapter 3:
Action Based
On The Interpretation

A week went by and there was no action of consequence. Renata started their afternoon together noticing and indicating to Sonia that Forty-Seven (FTSV) closed the week at $39.03. Sonia seemed unperturbed by the paper loss.

Renata calculated that the $45,740 amount was now worth $39,030. That was a quick loss of over $6,500 in a week! But she noticed the calmness with which Sonia took the news. Even more shocking to Renata was the cool aloofness with which Sonia continued the week's work of checking on other charts that Renata brought up to Sonia.

Among the new stocks that seemed to garner an incredible amount of interest was a stock called Myokardia (MYOK). Similar to the index finger tracing exercise Renata performed with Forty-Seven, Inc (FTSV), Sonia used her index finger to trace the price line for Myokardia (MYOK) with the assistance of Renata.

"This looks interesting. This Myokardia. Could you please take my finger and run it all along the price line for Myokardia?," asked Sonia.

Sonia wanted Renata to repeat the action for Myokardia a couple of times, as if Sonia was trying to memorize the price action on the chart of Myokardia. When they were at it for the second time, Renata began to see an upward price movement on Myokardia from her own eyes. She realized that she had never paid attention to price movements before in this simple manner.

Another week went by. This week Forty-Seven dropped a few dollars more in price and closed out the week at $36.87. Renata was getting very nervous for Sonia. *Almost nine thousand dollars in the hole!*

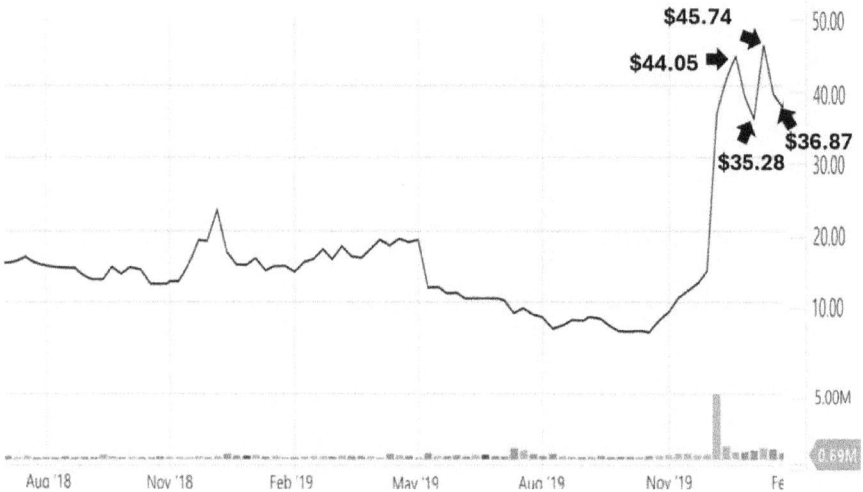

Chart 3.5

As they finished the week's work and reviewed the most recent week's action on Myokardia and on Forty-Seven, Renata broached the subject of the paper loss with Sonia.

"I am so nervous, Sonia. You are losing almost nine thousand dollars on this stock, Forty-Seven. It is heading the wrong way!"

"I cannot do anything, so I do not worry about things I cannot do anything about."

"But Sonia! This is a nine thousand dollars loss. Aren't you concerned?"

"My dear Renata, I have been at this a long time. This stock can swing and dance all it wants, up and down, just so long as it does not hit my sell-stop price of $31.75. If you fish, you will understand. You give the fish a line. She can go against you for a while. And then you reel her in towards you. That is the nature of the game. A game of patience."

Renata was deep in thought as she headed out of Sonia's house that evening. She got into her car in the driveway and sat quietly deep in thought. *What is Sonia seeing in these stocks that she is so interested in them?*

As she was about to start her ignition, she heard violin music coming out of Sonia's house. It was very pretty. *Sonia is so good at playing the violin!*

The following Friday Renata was running a few minutes behind and called Sonia to inform her of a few minutes' delay. Sonia was not happy.

"I need you here today, Renata. I called my broker, and he said that Forty-Seven is making a new high. I need to take some action, and I would really like to have your eyes here with me."

"Please do not worry, Sonia. I am running no more than ten minutes late. I will be there on time. I will be there twenty minutes before the market closes. Would that be enough time for you?"

"Yes, Renata, who is plenty of time. But if you run into any more delays, please call me right away. Then I will have to call my broker and keep him on the phone until the last few minutes of the market close."

Twenty minutes before the market closed Renata walked into Sonia's living room and walked over to the table where Sonia had a pot of coffee and two empty coffee cups waiting. Renata apologized for the delay and was on her laptop within seconds. Forty-Seven (FTSV) was trading at $49 a share.

"Oh, wow! It went up a lot this week! From $36.87 last Friday to $49 today, in just one week!" exclaimed Renata.

"Yes, I have to now buy more. That is why I needed you here today on time. I know there was no way to know this, and I know you were not late on purpose today. But I was getting a bit anxious about you arriving late today," responded Sonia but her voice did not reflect any of the anxiety she referred to. She was calm as ever.

"What am I doing today with Forty-Seven? What am I looking for?"

"Let us keep watching its price, Renata, as we come towards the market close. I need to see that it clearly closes above $45.74. Wait till 3:50 pm and let me know where the price is at that point."

As they waited for the minutes to tick by, both Sonia and Renata sat in silence, each sipping on their cup of coffee. The wait seemed to go by slowly. Sonia was in total silence. As the time to act arrived, she checked with Renata for the prevailing price for Forty-Seven stock. It was still at $49.00.

Sonia called her broker. After the usual authentication process, Sonia calmly called in her order.

Buy 1000 FTSV at market

Change sell-stop to 2000 FTSV at $33.18 GTC

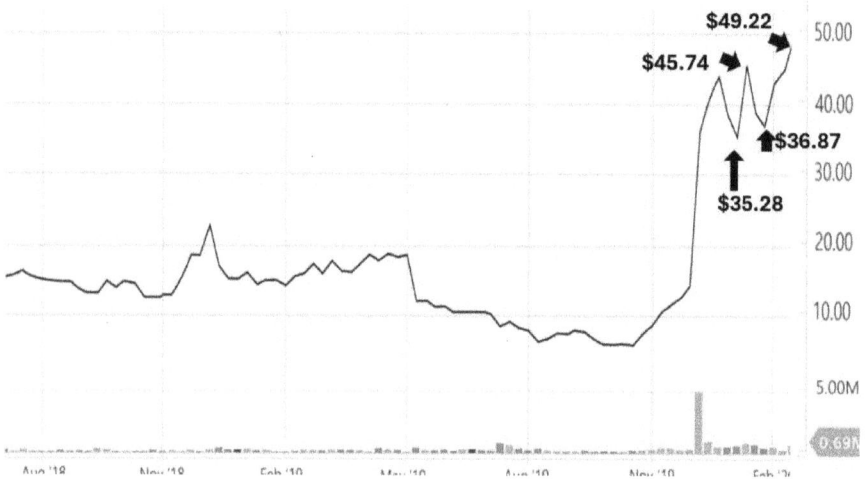

Chart 3.6

A few seconds later she hung up the phone and informed Renata that she got filled at $49.22. And pushed her *Journal Of Trade Secrets* towards Renata and asked her to enter the trade right under the prior entry in that journal. Now Renata could see both entries, one under the prior entry.

1000 FTSV @ $45.74

Total committed = $45,740

Stop price $31.75, worst-case scenario loss = $45,740 - $31,750 = $13,990

1000 FTSV @ $49.22

Total committed = $49,220 + $45,740 = $94,960

Stop price $33.18, worst-case scenario loss = $94,960 - $66,360 = ($28,600)

Renata was stunned. Sonia was willing to lose $28,600 on her bet that Forty-Seven would be going up in price. She must really have some serious conviction. What does she know about this stock that no one else does? The investigative journalist in her wanted to dig into this. But her current time commitments did not allow her to spend much time on this. Renata made a mental note to check into Forty-Seven as soon as time allowed her.

The following Friday, around midday, Renata received a phone call from Sonia. Renata was finishing up a report she was working on for a client as a freelancer. It was only noon, and it was not yet time to head over to Sonia's. A little bit concerned, Renata answered the phone.

"Hi Renata! I am so sorry to call you, but I just wanted to make sure you will be here on time today. Please do not think that I have lost confidence in your professionalism, I know you were late last week due to circumstances, and it was just a one-time thing. Today's market action on Forty-Seven dictates a certain type of action. I really need you here today."

"It is no issue, Sonia. Please don't worry, I will be there on time. Not to worry."

Renata arrived on time, exactly at 3:30 pm that Friday. Having settled herself down with her laptop open, she turned around to Sonia and finally asked her, "What is going on today? You seemed a bit anxious on your phone earlier today… ….Oh my goodness! I see now! The stock is $57! It jumped so much today. What is going on? Are you thinking of selling to lock in your profit? Let me see, this is almost $20,000 profit in just a few weeks! You did great, Sonia!"

Sonia smiled and sipped on her coffee and shook her head.

"Actually, I am looking to buy more. So, I need your help. What was the day's low price today?"

"Huh? Hmm…let me see. The day's low price today was $54.37, Sonia."

After that exchange between the two, Sonia went back to asking Renata to assist her in going over the week's action on other stocks, including the action on Myokardia. There were a handful of stocks that Sonia asked Renata to place on a list she called, "The Perfect Watchlist." Myokardia was on it, as were a few other stocks. The number of stocks that Sonia wanted to watch every weekend had increased from just Forty-Seven (FTSV) to now more than a handful of stocks.

Soon enough it was time for Sonia to call her broker. And Sonia went ahead and placed her order.

Buy 2000 FTSV at the market

A few seconds later, she ended the phone call and looked at Renata and said, "I got filled at $58.00. That was the day's closing price as well. Now it is time for you to help me add this position to my Journal Of Trade Secrets, Renata."

Renata picked the *Journal Of Trade Secrets* that was laying on the table. She opened the page of her previous entry. As Sonia narrated, Renata wrote down the trade entries.

Buy 2000 FTSV at $58.00

Amount committed = $116,000

Total Committed = $116,000 + $45,740 + $49,220 = $210,960

Move sell-stop to $48.60.

Worst-case scenario = $210,960 – (4,000 x $48.60) = ($16,560)

Renata thought to herself in her head, while being professional and detached from it all on the outside. *But why? You had twenty grand profit and now you are facing sixteen grand in loss if you are wrong! That is a swing of thirty-six thousand dollars!*

Renata was confused at first, but quickly noticed that the lower the dollar amount committed, the higher the percentage of the dollar amount risked. And the higher the commitment, the lower the dollar percentage risked. *Maybe there was a method to Sonia's madness after all.*

Chart 3.7

The following Monday, Renata woke up at 6:00 am. She went for her daily morning run. When she got back home, she showered, and she was getting ready to have breakfast, and she heard a ping on her phone. She walked towards her phone and picked it up. It was an alert she had set up for Forty-Seven, Inc. Ever since she started working for Sonia, she had placed an alert for any breaking news about Forty-Seven, Inc.

What she saw on her phone was shocking. It read in bold print, "Gilead Sciences has agreed to acquire Forty-Seven, Inc., an immuno-oncology company, for $4.9 billion or $95.50/share ….."

Renata sat down stunned. She took her phone and ran some numbers on her phone calculator, imagining what she would enter in Sonia's Journal Of Trade Secrets.

Bought 4000 FTSV = total committed $210,960

Sold 4000 FTSV @ $95.50 = total received $382,000

Profit = $382,000 - $210,960 = $171,040

How the heck did Sonia know about this in advance? I wonder if Forty-Seven Inc.'s charts can offer any clues.

91

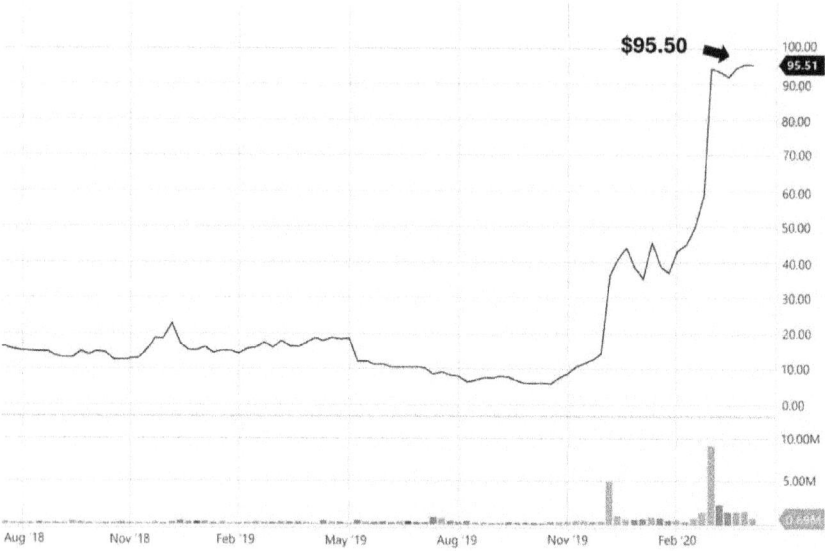

Chart 3.8

Chart 3.9

Chapter 4:
The Investigative Reporter

Having seen the stock operations run by Sonia, Renata Wierink's investigative mind wanted to dig into Gilead and Forty-Seven. She was new to the field of investigative journalism and there was much that she could not unearth. But despite her lack of experience and resources, she still came up with a short article. She did not share it with anyone. It was for her own personal records, perhaps to learn from in the ensuing years. It read:

When Did Forty-Seven Become $95.50?

The Biotech Sector had entered a new era. Like life in general in the new century, the sector was experiencing a sort of outsourcing. The big pharmaceuticals were too rigid and too set in their ways to allow for innovative thought and experiments. Most of the innovations were coming from smaller units and labs. As if science was being outsourced.

It was 2015, when a small and new young biotechnology company called Forty-Seven, Inc. came to the market. Forty-Seven was working on a new drug called Magrolimab. Magrolimab was the new hope to treat blood cancers like myelodysplastic syndrome (MDS) and acute myeloid leukemia (AML) by targeting a specified protein called CD47 which is used by cancer cells to evade the immune system.

Aside from the trials in MDS and AML, Magrolimab is also undergoing testing in three solid tumor types (colorectal, ovarian, and bladder), non-Hodgkin lymphoma, and diffuse large B-cell lymphoma. Each of these affects numerous children and adults around the world and this drug may help alleviate the suffering from these terrible cancers.

Soon the FDA gave Magrolimab a fast-track designation and Forty-Seven started trials on human patients. Enter Gilead Sciences Inc., a larger and more established pharmaceutical company who already had an interest in expanding its oncology portfolio. Hearing about Forty-Seven's potentially groundbreaking drug Magrolimab and its aim to help treat a variety of cancers, Gilead wanted to add the company and its product to its existing pipeline.

The process of acquisition was fraught with numerous negotiations and strategic maneuvering. This is common in any merger or acquisition as both companies want to get the best deal that they can to ensure employees, products, and research are all valued accordingly and paid fairly for.

Once this news hit, Forty Seven's stock showed rapid growth in two weeks, going from sub $15 a share to just over $40 a share. This had been an amazing transformation as Forty Seven's stock had been as low as $6 per share and mostly hovered just below $20 a share till then.

The initial meeting between Gilead and Forty Seven took place just after the positive data regarding Magrolimab came to light. And just before Christmas, both companies had their first talk through specialists of mergers and acquisitions (M&A) at the headquarters of Gilead Sciences where the executives created the foundation of the agreement and initial offering.

A second meeting took place in early February. That meeting was so promising that Gilead was adamant and a lot more focused on acquiring Forty-Seven, and later that same day, a written proposal was created and sent to Forty-Seven Inc. to acquire the young company. The initial offer was turned down as Forty-Seven wanted more than the offered $57.50 a share.

Gilead was surprised. This was February 2020. Gilead knew the market was facing headwinds. The knowledge of Covid-19 being on its way and creating havoc was quite well-known in the biotech sector. Though it would take weeks and several months before the public at large would face the Covid-19 crisis. Given the expected downward pressure on the financial markets, Gilead thought their offer was quite generous.

Wanting to show the company's worth, Forty-Seven had an ace up their sleeve as they sent over more private clinical data to entice Gilead Sciences to present a larger offer. Although the data was private it can only be assumed that it was positive in how the drug trials and testing were going.

After receiving the data, both the companies communicated often over emails, text, and telephone. Sources say the data that was sent over was of great interest to Gilead, and a new offer would be created with this information in mind. Since progress had been going well with the *potential* wonder drug, the valuation for buying the company would be re-examined.

Gilead, after much talk within itself, came back with an increased offer of $68.50 a share.

However, in a twist, someone had leaked the news of Gilead taking over Forty Seven to Bloomberg, a business and market news organization, which reported on the deal. Once word got out that Gilead, a major player in the medical industry, was seeking to acquire Forty-Seven because of its potential wonder drug, the stock prices for Forty-Seven shot up. And this forced Gilead's hand.

Gilead and Forty-Seven met again briefly to discuss the leak to Bloomberg, how that impacted the stock price rise for Forty-Seven, and what the implications would be for any upcoming offerings. Still respectful of each other, their back and forth was fruitful in providing Gilead Sciences with a path forward. One that would hopefully end with the acquisition of Forty-Seven.

Arguing for an increase wasn't the hard part as most within Gilead knew they would have to bring more to the table, the hard part was setting the price, one that was within a fair value range, but nothing to break the bank. After some internal talk, Gilead came back and raised their offer to $77 a share.

Forty-Seven came back and said, 'No thanks,' which shocked Gilead Sciences. With more meetings, and more late nights, Gilead Sciences scrambled to work out how to deal with this process going forward.

With the last offer turned down, and with one final meeting, all of it prompted one final push from Gilead Sciences to offer Forty-Seven $95.50 a share, turning this into a whopping $4.9 billion deal. Forty-Seven's stock shot up 61% after the agreement.

In interviews after the deal went through, both the companies had some words to share. After such a monumental deal it was obvious that those in the industry wanted to see what was on their mind, the thoughts they had in the process. Instead, both entities remained sparse on words but offered nice things to say about each other's company.

"Magrolimab complements our existing work in hematology, adding a non-cell therapy program that complements our pipeline of cell therapies for hematological cancers," said Gilead Science Inc.

But who leaked the potential acquisition to Bloomberg? Obviously, it was the one with the most to gain.

Postscript: In 2024, FDA halted the use of Magrolimab for clinical studies due to some data showing increased risk of death. Gilead ended up scrapping Magrolimab. For Gilead, this turned out to be a dud of an investment. But it was not such a bad deal for Forty Seven, which made out quite well. It is clear that the leak to Bloomberg did not come from Gilead.

Case Study #4
You Could Do Everything Right
And Still Be Wrong

Chapter 1:
Be Silent, Be Sharp

Montgomery Sharp was doing his daily morning routine. He was staring at himself in the mirror. To be more precise, he was talking to himself in the mirror. He had just taken a few losses in a row in his stock trading operations. The losses were minimal. But when they occur in successive trades, even the most experienced operator faces doubts. Montgomery had faced situations like this before. He was an experienced operator. Early on it had been difficult to deal with successive losses. But as the years went by, and Montgomery learned about being a successful stock speculator and sharpened his speculating skills, he had developed a system to keep himself even keeled.

It is a cliché, but "not too high, not too low" were not just words. They were the key to Montgomery's success in the market. After the usual initial few years and cycles of losses interspersed with an occasional lucky win, Montgomery Sharp had come up with a routine of talking to himself in the mirror. He found that talking to others was self-defeating and made him distrust his own instincts, and he was liable to second-guess himself based on the words from others. He had come to understand that he had to keep away from other humans if he had any chance of success. But the solitary journey was a bit disconcerting and talking to himself helped. In fact, it helped him a lot, so much so that it had become a daily routine.

"MRTX jumped last week. Watch that stock now. If it shows the right kind of action, you know what to do. What happened in your recent trades have no bearing on the next trade. Remember, you have a short memory. Forget about the past trades. Take a deep breath. Inhale. Exhale. See? All forgotten. Stay in the present, where your feet are."

That morning talking to himself in the mirror worked and Sharp forgot all about the prior losses. His mind and his eyes were focused on observing the price/volume action on Mirati Therapeutics (MRTX), a stock that had caught his eye. It was not ready yet to invite his funds, but it was on his radar. It did not take Mirati Therapeutics (MRTX) long to get Montgomery to make his first financial commitment to it.

It was November 2017. And Montgomery made his experimental buy in Mirati Therapeutics. It was just another biotech company among a sea of biotechs all chasing a blockbuster drug. Sharp was not all knowing in biotechs as some people are. He was smart in many ways, but he was really smart in the sense that he knew he was not the smartest. His approach to stock operations was quite simple.

The stock market is a roulette wheel. There are traps all over the place. When you come to a watering hole that is full of dollars, you will face all kinds of predators and prey. In an environment where many predators don't even know that they are preys themselves, Montgomery felt he had no chance to make money.

Every position he took, he took with the understanding that it was a position that would hit him with a loss. He placed a trade fully expecting to lose on the trade. This approach and mental programming had been developed after years and years of experience in the market. He had seen bull trends and bear trends. He had learned that you could lose in both. He had also learned that there was a small chance of winning but that was only possible in a bull trend. Winning in a bear trend was possible but only if you had mastered going short. But the profit potential in a shorting operation was not unlimited. A long position offered an opportunity to make many multiples of return on his commitment.

There was no reason to be in the market if big profits cannot be made. He had zero interest in taking all kinds of risks that come with the stock market to make a buck or two. If he could double or triple his money, only then did the stock interest him.

In many ways, everything about Montgomery Sharp's stock operation was a paradox. He hated risk but was willing to extend his line on the riskiest of stocks. That was the main reason for his love for biotechnology stocks. He had faced his share of losses on biotechs, but they were minimal when compared to the ludicrous profits he had made on biotechnology stocks.

He came to the market with the mindset that he was going to lose, as opposed to most people who come to the market in the hopes of making profits. He placed his trades with the mindset that it was a loss even before clicking on the "Place Your Order" button on his screen. Others did the same but with the *hope and expectation* of a win. He was only interested in buying a stock later in its move, as opposed to the human tendency and wish to try and get in early, before a move started. Most people could not deal with the volatile nature of biotechnology stocks, while Sharp wished for the volatility and wild swings. Those were the stocks that could make the big bucks. A wild stock is the one with the most room to run.

Montgomery placed his first experimental buy on Mirati Therapeutics. That weekend, he entered his trade in his *Book Of Trade Secrets*, a journal he kept of all his trades.

Bought 1,000 MRTX @ 15.75 Stop $11.52 GTC
Spent $15,750. Willing to lose $4,230.
Total Commitment = $15,750
Worst-Case Scenario = ($4,230)

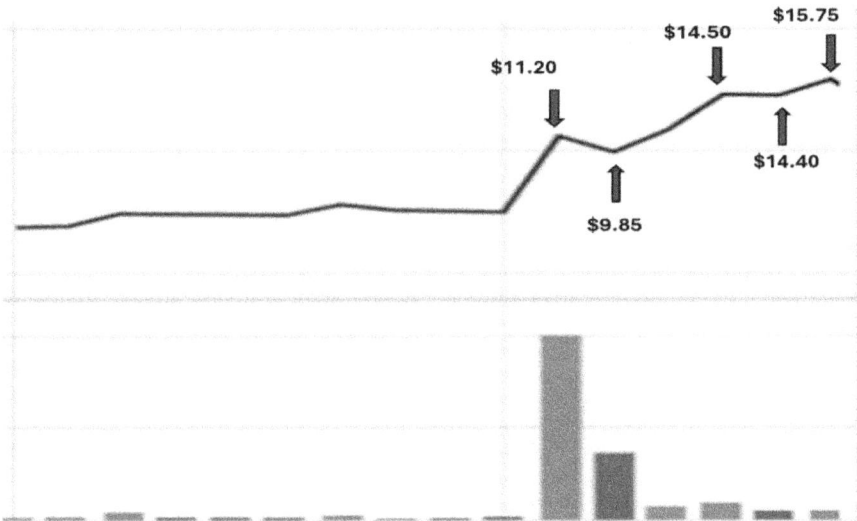

Chart 4.1

Chapter 2:
The Stock Tells The Story – Phase 1

The original breakout on Mirati Therapeutics had occurred in September 2017. Amazingly, Montgomery Sharp's entry into Mirati stock was two months later. Once again, the paradox of Montgomery's stock operation stood out. Most traders, the social media obsessed 24/7 cell phone wielding self-proclaimed experts, and the day trading crowd would have jumped on the stock in September. Many of them may have already closed out their original entry position.

For most active traders, it would seem as though Sharp's buy was made late. After all, Mirati had reacted to some positive results on its drug trials a couple months back. It was two months prior to Montgomery Sharp making his experimental buy that Mirati went from a $5 a share stock to over $11 a share within a week as a wild reaction to this news of positive drug trials.

For Montgomery it mattered not what the market, the crowd, or the media said or thought. He was only focused on what the stock actually did. His whole modus operandi was based on what actually happened. His was not an operation that relied on projections, predictions, expectations, mathematical models or computer programming or coding or some quantitative analysis. Montgomery Sharp was a stickler to his method and relied on himself and the stock with which he was speculating. His operation relied on *waiting*. A different kind of waiting. That was his edge.

Sharp had learned that time made money in the market. To him *time* meant spending time staying out of lousy markets. And when stocks start acting well, to find the stock that seems to be in a definite uptrend and to try and hold that stock for as long as possible, because time made the big money.

He found no need to research Mirati or the drugs it had in the pipeline. The stock itself told the story. No amount of research he could do would be any better than what the stock was messaging him through its price and volume action. The only risk he had was being shaken out of a great stock. His reasoning was simple. If the smartest people on the planet found a gem whose value was likely going to go up many-fold in the coming months or years, they will do all they can to grab as many of those gems as possible. Which means, they will create fake news to drive its price down artificially by scaring the less than smart folks to sell out. And when the less than smart people sold the gems, the smart people would gobble it all up. And when the value of that gem really starts to skyrocket, the only ones holding the gems would be the really smart people.

The smart people will shake out the less than smart ones. It happens all the time. Montgomery himself had fallen prey to shakeout more times than he cared to count. He did not know yet, but Mirati was going play the shakeout game with him like no other he had experienced before. The entire play would last for Montgomery Sharp from November 2017 to January 2021. That time frame of a little over three years was longer than any he had encountered before where he was hooked on one single solitary stock. He was under the impression that he had seen almost everything in the market. But with Mirati he relearned a lesson he had learned many times before. A stock will do the unthinkable. A $100 stock can fall below $1 a share. And $5 a share stock can run to $300 a share within a few months. He had seen and experienced both.

To most people it would feel like the most unimaginable and unbelievable stocks make the big runs. It is because people have inherent bias. Everyone looks at the potential stocks to buy with a bias. One might think that there is no bias, but it is always there. The very fact that one believes that they have no bias is an indication that they have a bias. Not actually having a bias and believing that one does not have a bias are two completely different things.

Sharp had accepted that despite the decades of experience, he was not without some form of bias. The only difference now was that Sharp was more aware and accepting of the fact that he had bias, a hidden bias, a bias that was not evident to him. But it was there, hidden, out of sight and submerged inside, away from his self-awareness.

In his attempt at becoming better at speculating in stocks, Montgomery had spent plenty of time in front of a mirror, talking to his reflection, instilling self-discipline. Moreover, he had spent decades perfecting the art of speculation in the stock market. But life in the stock market business is a never-ending learning lesson. Every cycle is different. Every stock is different.

With Mirati everything started off quite as expected for Montgomery. After his first commitment, Mirati offered a second chance to buy. Like clockwork, Sharp went about his systematic approach and placed his next trade. He had forgotten the successive losses he had faced in the most recent string of trades. He relied on his gut instinct, an instinct he had developed over the many years of operations.

Bought 1,000 MRTX @ 17.25 Stop $11.52 GTC

Spent $17,500. Willing to lose $5,730.

Total Shares now held = 2,000

Commitment = $15,750 + $17,250 = $33,000

Worst-Case Scenario = $33,000 – (2000 x $11.52) = ($9.960)

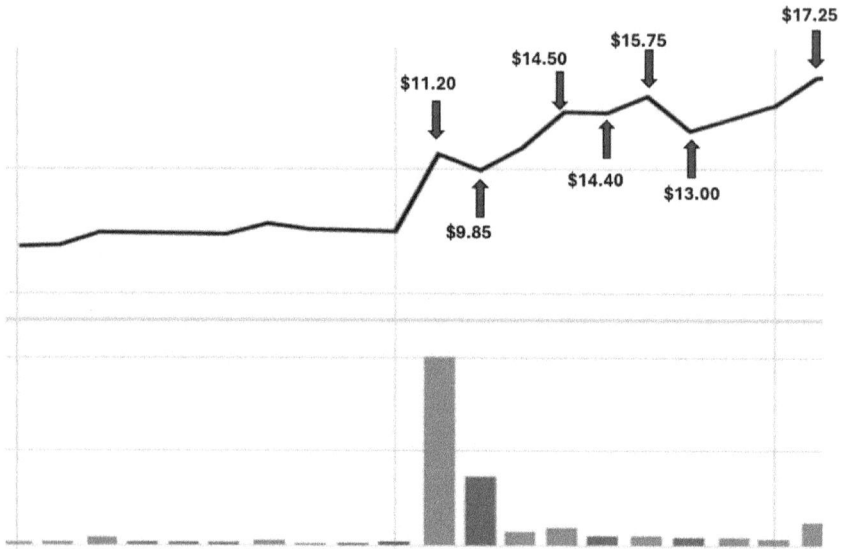

Chart 4.2

He wrote down his trade in his journal. He stopped for a moment and looked at the numbers in his *Book Of Trade Secrets* and thought he might have overextended a bit; a bit more than he would have liked. But the conviction within him was strong. A little bit later, something told him to extend his line even more. The stock made yet another new high at $17.80. And without thought, Montgomery placed his next trade, and promptly entered the details of the trade in his journal. His stop moved up and that was all that he truly cared about.

Bought 2,000 MRTX @ 17.80 Stop $12.92 GTC

Spent $35,600. Willing to lose $9,760.

Total Shares now held = 4,000

Commitment = $15,750 + $17,250 + $35,600 = $68,600

Worst-Case Scenario = $68,600 - (4000 x $12.92) = ($16.920)

Chart 4.3

The next morning, he spoke to himself, "Well, now, that was a bigger than ideal worst-case scenario. But I had no choice. She is making a higher high, and a higher low. My price is rising, as is my sell-stop. No choice. I had to play the game the right way and make my move."

As days turned into weeks, and as time passed, the stock continued making new highs. Before he knew it, there was a series of eleven successive weeks of a higher closing price that followed. And soon it closed to a new high price of $29.60. The stock had run from $17.80 to $29.60 without a reaction. And Sharp was just bracing for a reaction now. After eleven straight weeks of higher and higher closing prices, the reaction was imminent. That was the obvious part. But just how big a reaction was the unknown.

He didn't have to wait long as the reaction came about the very next week. But only lasted for two weeks as the stock pegged a low of the reaction at $28.45, a minimal reaction, before its upward move continued. It made a new higher high at $34.60.

Chart 4.4

Montgomery Sharp looked at the chart and looking at the new stop now being indicated at $22.76. The sell-stop had jumped from $12.92 to $22.76. He ran some numbers. He decided to go for it. He made a big buy, big enough to be bold, but still within reason to not lose on a winning stock. That weekend he entered his trade in his journal.

Bought 1,600 MRTX @ 34.60 Stop $22.76 GTC

Spent $55,360.

Total Shares now held = 5,600

Commitment = $15,750 + $17,250 + $35,600 + $55,360= $123,960

Worst-Case Scenario = (5,600 x $22.76) – ($123,960) = +3,496

Sharp's commitment at the final buy was such that even in the worst-case scenario, if his stop got triggered, he would not take a loss. He looked at himself in the mirror that weekend. *She was acting the way a winner acts. I had to be bold and take that aggressive step and make the big commitment. But protecting myself such that I would not lose on a winning stock. Now just wait and see. She will let you know if she wants to dance with you or not.*

As is usual in the stock market, just as Montgomery took a big commitment, the stock reacted. And the reaction was swift and sharp. His account value was $193,760 when the price was $34.60. The quick reaction took the price of Mirati from $34.60 to $26.05 during four consecutive weeks of downward price close. Most people would pay attention to their account value daily. At $26.05 Montgomery's account value dropped from $193,760 to $145,880 during the four-week reaction.

But Sharp played by his own rules, and he never paid attention to the account value fluctuations. He had learned years ago that it was for more important to play the game the right way without paying attention to the score. Paying attention to the score distracts traders from the discipline.

Chart 4.5

Sharp was allowed by his stock to hang with it for about four or five more months before his stop at $44.37 got triggered. Along the way his stop prices kept moving up from $22.76 to $44.37. When he was stopped out at $44.37, his account value was $248,472. He had doubled his money in eleven or twelve months. It was when he entered his trades in his *Book Of Trade Secrets* that he realized the profit he had made.

Total Shares held = 5,600

Commitment = $15,750 + $17,250 + $35,600 + $55,360= $123,960

Amount received when stopped out = 5600 x $44.37 = $248,472

Profit = $248,472 - $123,960 = $124,512

I doubled my money! From October 2017 to October 2018.

Most folks would have looked at the chart and asked why he had not gotten out when the stock was above $60 a share. And Montgomery would have replied curtly that the rules that got him in the way he got in, also got him out the way he got out. And that only novices, and those who falsely brag, look at a chart and claim to be able to catch the bottom and the top.

Chapter 3:
The Stock Gets Confused – Phase 2

Montgomery knew very well that more often than not humans get confusing signals from the stock market. The content creators have a field day, day after day, creating content to satisfy the human need to know the answers of which way the market is going to move. One can find an article or a prediction to suit every mindset. If one is a perennial bull, there will be a content creator who will provide content to satisfy the reader's mindset. For the doom and gloom bear, there will be another content provider that will do the job. And for the entire range of spectrum of mindsets there are niche content creators. The only one that makes a profit through all cycles is the content creator. The speculator stays out of lousy markets and foregoes many years of potential wins, knowing very well that the odds are always stacked against him. In bad markets, the odds get even worse. He is only active in good conditions. It could mean being active for maybe three out of any ten-year time frame. And the three years would not even be all together. It could be that he is active for months on three separate time frames within those ten years.

Speculators like Montgomery Sharp wait and wait for long periods of time without any profits to show. But they also wait and wait without any losses to show either, by virtue of staying out of bad markets.

Sharp also had learned that humans are not the only ones confused by the market. Stocks themselves get confused sometimes. The currents are many and the direction of the currents are chaotic. Sometimes the stock gets stuck in a wave that does not let it breathe and the stock writhes and struggles to find its footing. Trying to catch stocks in such periods is fraught with shake-outs and big drawdowns. Sharp had his method to stay in the present and avoid situations like these. But no method of operation is fool proof. That was the situation that Montgomery found himself in during the second phase of Mirati's journey.

After he got stopped out, he looked around at other stocks and the prospects were slim. The content creators and the various forms of media were touting a bull trend. But stocks were singing a different tune for Montgomery Sharp. He was not liking very many stocks. He went on a vacation for a while. But as was his habit, even on a vacation he would check in every weekend on his watchlist of stocks to see if anything interesting was happening. Nothing was jumping out at him.

He kept coming back to Mirati. Of all the stocks out there, Mirati still continued to act as if it wanted to get back on the saddle, and ride again. Eventually, after several months Mirati offered a signal to buy again. But Montgomery was circumspect. He had seen several traders make a killing on one trade and on the very next trade give it all back and more.

He looked at the chart again. It looked to Montgomery as if Mirati wanted to re-assert itself and make higher highs. After his phase 1 operations had ended, a new phase was beginning.

Chart 4.6

And Mirati wanted him to buy. But he was wary of the temptation. And decided to embark on this second phase of Mirati's move with a small test buy.

Chart 4.7

The stock was clearly wanting to move higher. He just was not sure that the general conditions were right enough to support a big move. Very few new highs were showing up elsewhere. But he had no choice but to listen to the stock and he went ahead with his first experimental buy with a small 200 share buy. And immediately wrote down the details of the trade in his *Book Of Trade Secrets*.

Bought 200 MRTX @ $70.44 Stop $53.28 GTC

Spent $14,088. Willing to lose $3,432.

In Sharp's mind, the $3,432 loss he was willing to face was a fee he was willing to pay Mirati to see if she could offer him guidance, if she was really ready to make another big move. As the weeks rolled on, Mirati seemed somewhat confused, and Montgomery played along with her.

In the media all the usual shenanigans were going on. *Mirati has topped out. No, it has not, look at its drug trials. And look at its pipeline of products* *ready for FDA submissions, FDA approvals and blah blah blah. Our price target is $150. No, our price target is $130. No, these FDA approvals will be rejected, so our target is $30.* It never ended, and Sharp never paid attention. Mirati went through yet another quarter of earnings release. To Sharp it mattered none. He was only listening to the stock via its chart.

Chart 4.8

Soon Mirati made another set of a higher high and a higher low. And Sharp had no choice but to go ahead and make his move. He ended up buying an additional 75 shares. He wrote his trade in his journal again. He did not want to face more than $5,000 or so in losses on the second phase of his operations.

Bought 75 MRTX @ $76.31 Stop $54.34 GTC

Spent $5,723.25

Total shares = 200 + 75 = 275

Total Committed =14,088 + 5,723.25 = $19,811.25

Total Potential loss if stopped out = $19,811.25 − (275 x $54.34) = ($4,867.75)

The next morning, while he was having breakfast, he decided that he was not going to risk more than the current amount he had resigned to losing on the current second phase of Mirati operations. He figured that should Mirati really want to make a run again; she will offer him plenty of opportunities. As some more time passed, Mirati offered Sharp the following look as shown by the chart below.

Chart 4.9

At each of the new price highs of $76.31 and $76.74 and again at $99.77, he had no choice but to just sit tight and wait. It was when Mirati closed above $100 for the first time and pegged a new all-time high at $101.44 that Sharp seemed convinced that perhaps Mirati was really on a new serious uptrend. He ran his numbers and checked his new rising trailing stop was now at $75.41. A figure at which, if his stop got hit, he would be at breakeven and would not be facing any losses. This was an encouraging sign for him.

Now he was mentally getting ready to play it out, and decided should Mirati offer a new opportunity to buy, he would go in with the idea that he will be willing to lose $10,000 on the next commitment. And just when he was ready to go in with a bigger commitment, Mirati turned around and sank to his sell-stop and told him not to be involved with her. His second phase of the operations had come to an end.

Chart 4.10

All those weeks he danced with Mirati and he had nothing to show for as profits. But then he had not taken a loss either as he had broken even, with a small pocket change of a little over $900. He entered his trade as he was stopped out.

Total shares = 200 + 75 = 275

Total Committed = 14,088 + 5,723.25 = $19,811.25

Stopped out, total received 275 x 75.41 = $20,737.75

Walked away with some pocket change of $926.50

No Loss!

Chapter 4:
Avoid The Confusion – Phase 3

Montgomery Sharp had met his match many times before. Many a stock operation in his past had thrown him off kilter. Those stocks that truly baffled him were the ones that taught him the best lessons. He thought he had learned many lessons and was well prepared to deal with any move a stock made. And yet, he couldn't figure Mirati out.

Yes, he had doubled his money during the first phase of the Mirati stock operations. And yes, he had not taken a loss during the second phase of the Mirati stock operations. But here she was, throwing more decoys and traps. Montgomery Sharp was staring at himself in the mirror again. He had been watching Mirati since the end of his trades during Phase 2 of his operations

He had been in the right stock at the right time, with the right commitments. But she just would not dance with him. Every time he warmed up and was rearing to dance, she would walk away. It was frustrating to him, but he was mentally disciplined. Long years in the market had seasoned him.

He stared at himself in the mirror for a moment. Then he looked down at the chart of Mirati he had printed out with his annotations.

Chart 4.11

He had to force his mind to push away the thought, a normal human thought, that came into his mind. *If I had just held on to my 5600 shares from Phase 1 operations, it would be worth $719,000! I sold out too early for just $248,000!*

He realized that he had to get into this next phase, Phase 3 of the Mirati price move. But he also knew that he had to play the game the right way. No shortcuts, no fancy stuff. He knew he could not afford to try and think he was smarter than her. She had already proven what Montgomery already knew, that the stock is always smarter. There was no chance of outsmarting her. Just find a way to dance with her, try to be in sync with her. Do not place your left foot forward when she wishes you to place your right foot forward.

It was easy to see and easier to say that his stops were almost close to lows of what ended up being a reaction rather than end of the trend. But Montgomery Sharp would be the first to acknowledge that in real-time there was no way for him to tell or anyone else to tell. There are no crystals balls and there is no holy grail. All there was at his disposal was discipline, a disciplined method he had developed and relied upon based on his long long years of experience trading in the markets. He had used Yogi Berra's famous quote, "Baseball is 90% mental and the other half physical" and applied it to the stock market to remind himself of the challenges even for the most disciplined. Montgomery looked at his reflection in the mirror and said to himself, "Remember, success in the stock market is 90% mental and the other half pure luck!"

And he then resolved himself to play the next phase with utmost discipline, playing the game the right way without paying attention to the score. He had to place his trades without regard to the daily and weekly swings of his account value.

He looked at the chart of Mirati again and concluded that he could not buy it yet. There just was not a clear sell-stop visible, not yet. He decided to pass on buying at the current new high of $128.43. *She is not offering a clear view of where to place my stop yet.*

He was now determined to learn to read her. To find a way to be in sync with her so that she would be willing to dance with him, until she was exhausted. That would mean he would be able to dance with her until the end, the end of her energy to keep making new highs. He waited for weeks, and true to form Mirati headed downwards after making that latest new high.

Chart 4.12

Sharp sat down at his desk with the most up-to-date chart of Mirati printed. He then went ahead and marked in the parts where he had carried out both the Phase 1 and the Phase 2 operations. He marked the latest high at $128.43. Then marked in the prior low at $73.55 and the new latest low at $71.71. He could feel it in his gut, he had danced with her for two sets of time periods, Phase 1, and Phase 2. He had learned her tendencies.

He looked at the two numbers, as pegged by the two most recent lows, $73.55 and $71.71. He felt she was shaking out folks. But he was not 100% sure. To test his gut feeling, he said to himself, "Last time I was willing to lose $5,000 and ended up coming out $900 ahead. Let me risk that $5000 plus the $900 pocket change, a total of $5,900 now and let me see what she says." And placed the trade to buy at $71.71. He wrote down his numbers in his *Book Of Trade Secrets*.

119

Buy 1070 MRTX at $71.71, Sell Stop $66.20 GTC

Commitment = 1070 x $71.71 = $76,729

Worst-case stop triggered at $66.20, would give me = 1070 x $66.20=
$70,834

Most I would lose = $76,729 - $70,834 = ($5,895)

He made his move. Now he had to wait for Mirati to make its move before he could decide what to do next. Quite soon after he made his move, Mirati started her dance. This time Montgomery was in sync, and he was ready. And then began a series of moves for a period of nine consecutive months that even Montgomery Sharp was amazed.

It started with the first entry Montgomery had made with a willingness to face a maximum loss of $5,895. Soon after that, Mirati made a set of higher highs and higher lows. Montgomery looked at the chart.

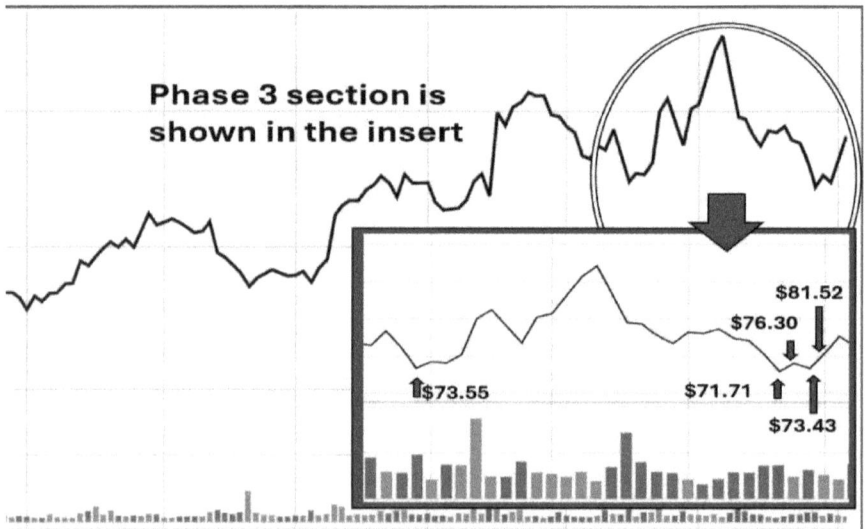

Chart 4.13

From a of $71.71, Mirati pegged a high at $76.30, immediately reacting to $73.43. There was nothing that warranted any action from Montgomery's point of view. He needed more information, a better view. It was when Mirati pegged a higher high at $81.52, it was clear to him that Mirati was willing to dance with him.

He wanted to wait. He felt good. She was acting right. She seemed to be willing to dance. But this was just the first step. He wanted to see what her second step was.

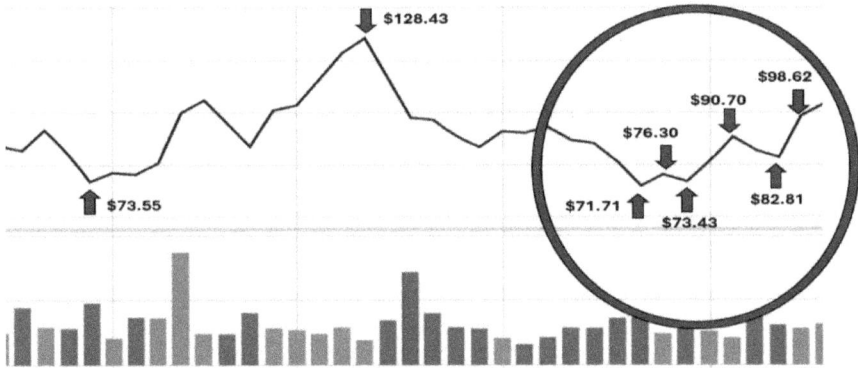

Chart 4.14

Montgomery printed the Mirati chart and circled the part of the chart he wanted to focus on. As soon as Mirati made another set of higher high and higher low, he decided to make his next purchase. His stop now moved up from the prior stop of $66.20 to $78.67. He ran some numbers and came up with the following trade, which he wrote down in his journal.

Buy 430 MRTX @ $98.62, Stop at $78.67 GTC

Commitment = $42,406.60

Total shares = 1070 + 430 = 1500

Total commitment = $76,729.70 + $42,406.60 =$119,136.30

If stop hit in the worst case, I receive =1500 x $78.67 = $118,005

Worst case, my loss = $119,136.30 - $118,005 = ($1,131.30)

Montgomery's thinking was that if indeed he was in sync with Mirati, it should be proven by his improving account condition. Since his first buy in Phase 3 would have resulted in a loss of $5,895 had his stop been hit, his loss should decrease with increasing commitment and rising stop price. Hence, he made his calculations such that his new worst-case scenario would have resulted in a loss of $1,131.30, a much lower loss than the original loss in the worst-case scenario of $5,895.

Yet again Montgomery had to wait. He knew that waiting was the key to winning in the stock market, and he had no qualms about waiting. When the waiting proved to be hard, he always had himself to talk to. He found talking to his own reflection in mirror grounded him, avoiding any distractions from the vast amount of noise in the market. He had stopped reading newspapers, stopped paying attention to CNBC and the noise his television made, and he was never a fan of social media. Anything that was connected to a human being on the other end was to be avoided. He avoided webinars, seminars, conferences, and any interaction with another human if the human was connected to the stock market. All his social interaction was, by design, only with those who never talked about the market.

A few weeks later, Montgomery was ready for his next move, which was purely based on the move made by Mirati. Again, he had the printed chart and studied it in his hand as he stared at the stock chart. Looking at the numbers, he pegged his new rising stop at $92.40, talking to himself and thinking out loud that Mirati was in a confirmed trend now. He placed his next trade.

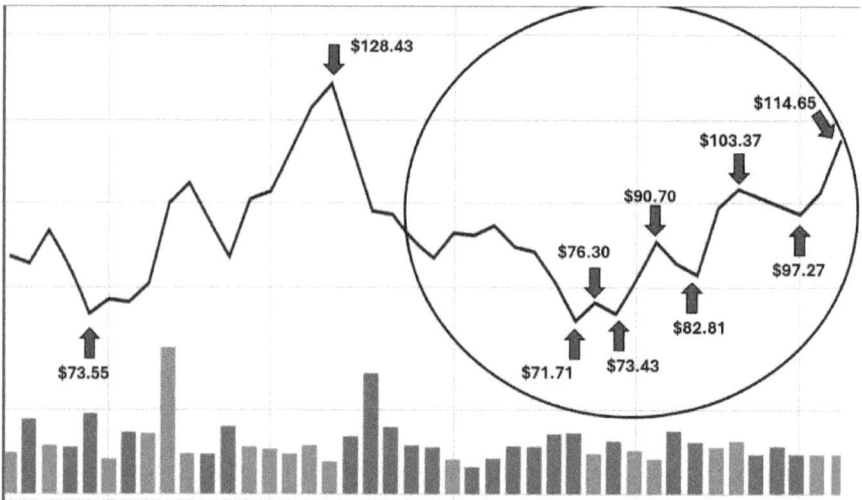

Chart 4.15

Buy 875 MRTX at $114.65, Sell stop $92.40 GTC
Total shares = 1500 + 875 = 2,375
Committed = 875 x 114.65 = $100,318.75
Total committed = $119,136.30 + $100,318.75 = $219,455.05
Worst-case scenario = 2375 shares x $92.40 = $219,450
Ha ha ha…fully committed and in the worst-case I would lose $5!

Montgomery Sharp felt good. He had been able to place over two hundred thousand dollars in Mirati, and in the worst-case scenario his risk was just $5! The price of a drink. But he knew that the next move Mirati was to make was going to be crucial in determining what he himself would do in reaction to Mirati's move. For a few weeks Mirati seemed to make a set of new highs and new higher lows, but Sharp just did not get a good feel for making a new move. So, he waited, he needed a little more room, he needed Mirati to make another move before he could react. Soon he saw Mirati's next move, and that gave him plenty of information to go ahead and make his final commitment in Mirati.

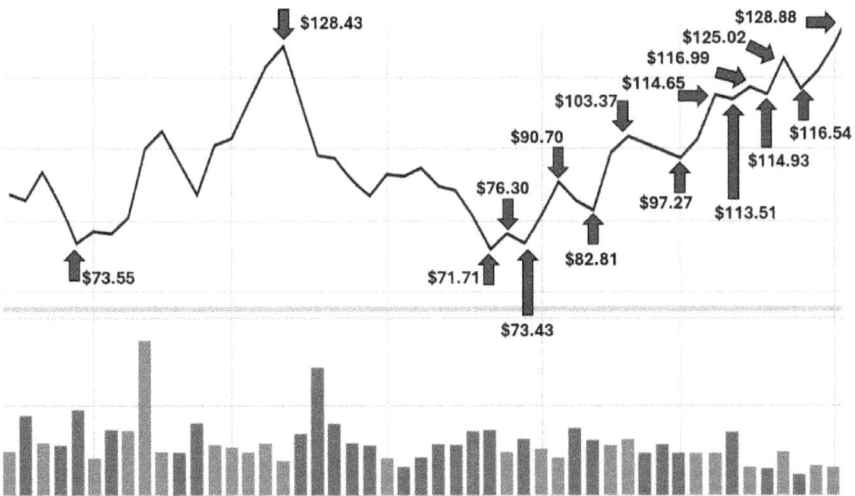

Chart 4.16

Montgomery ran his numbers and decided to make this his one final buy, as he sensed that Mirati's dance was now in full swing, nearing its peak energy. Sooner or later, she will stop dancing, and it would be time to go home. But not yet, she still had enough to keep going. And he then placed his final buy.

Buy 2000 MRTX at $128.88 Sell Stop $110.71 GTC
Commitment = $257,760
Total committed = $219,455.05 + $257,760 = $477,215.05
Total shares = 2375 + 2000 = 4375
Worst case scenario = 4375 x $110.71 = $484,356.25
If my stop get hit, I will take a loss of $7,141.20

Montgomery considered this to be a small loss compared to the amount he had committed. The stock kept rising, and he kept moving his stop higher and higher, trailing behind the rising stop as Mirati continued its march upward, above $140, and then above $160, and so on. He was able to wait with Mirati for an additional six months before Mirati ended the dance, forcing Montgomery to go home.

His rising stop kept rising and rising until eventually it got hit at $215.54 and his position in Mirati was liquidated.

Montgomery looked at his account value finally. And he saw himself writing in his journal.

Phase 3 MRTX
Sold 4375 shares MRTX at $215.54 = $942,987.50
Total Committed = $477,215.05
Profit = $465,772.45

Chart 4.17

Case Study #5
A Mind Is A Terrible Thing
To Use In The Stock Market

Chapter 1:
The Smart Harper

Dr. Curtis Harper was a believer in science. He was a believer in experiments. His belief in experimenting, running drug trials and the results and that the data from the drug trials can really benefit the human suffering from disease was about as strong as in any scientist.

Dr. Harper's love for science had started a long time ago, when he was in elementary school. And the interest and the love and the belief in science just grew with each passing year. By the time high school came along, Harper was an ace student, and it was a given that he would pursue science in college.

He grew up in a middle-class family, and he did not have enough financial means to afford any of the top schools. He had great grades, a top student in his high school graduating class. He had aced all the aptitude tests including a perfect score on the SAT. His guidance counselor had urged him to apply to a couple to top schools despite Harper's reluctance.

"Mrs. Tenny, there is no way my family can afford to put me through four years of some of these schools. That is over two hundred grand for a bachelor's degree in science. Just not going to happen and I am not going to even ask my parents for such a huge sacrifice."

Mrs. Tenny, his counselor, and a woman in her sixties had seen all kinds of students. She calmly said, "Curtis, I never expected you to approach your parents. I am going to tell you what I have seen in my years and years in this job. There are openings and opportunities for kids like you. Believe me, I have seen many students go to top schools with unimaginable scholarships. If a school wants you badly enough, they will find a way.

"Think of it like a football scholarship at universities that attract top high school football talent from around the country. It is similar, not exactly the same, but similar. If a school wants you, they will find a way to get you there. Mention in your application and essays, without being explicit, that you come from a background of meagre financial means and paying for a university education out of pocket is not within your family's plans.

"I would suggest you pick two or three of the best schools in your intended field of study. And apply to them. The key is being understated and implicit in your indication that you come from a modest background. Your grades, your recommendations and your scores are top notch. Easily in the top one percentile of the country. You will be surprised at the doors that could potentially open up."

Mrs. Tenny had convinced him to apply to several of the top schools in biotechnology and applied microbiology, the field that Harper intended to study. A few months later, Curtis Harper received the news that he was accepted to Johns Hopkins, Stanford and to MIT, aside from a couple of the local state public universities. While most would have been elated, Harper being the scientist he was, could not muster up any enthusiasm as getting in was not the issue for him. Paying for the four years was a concern.

Mrs. Tenny caught Harper one day as he was on his way to the library and was passing past Mrs. Tenny's office. Her door was open, and she saw him walking by her door, he seemed to be deep in thought. She called him in to her office.

"Congratulations Curtis! I heard about your acceptances."

"Thank you, Mrs. Tenny," he said without much energy.

"I am glad to see that you are so excited! Anyone else would be smiling ear to ear."

"Mrs. Tenny, I know that it should a cause for joy, but I won't be able to afford it. So, what is the point in all of this?"

"Really? They have not even sent you a financial package. Just wait for a few more weeks and let us see what happens. But in the meantime, learn to appreciate the small wins along the journey, pat yourself on the back once in a while. This is quite an achievement!"

A few weeks later Harper received the financial packages that Mrs. Tenny was referring to. Stanford and MIT had offered a generous scholarship, but he still would have to pay for room and board. From his calculations he was looking at an expense of well over a hundred thousand dollars for the four years. It was out of question. Johns Hopkins on the other hand had offered a complete free ride, his tuition was free, his room-and-board was going to be paid via a fund established by a generous donor who favored biotechnology students.

Suddenly he felt free, he wanted to fly, set himself free to go anywhere his mind desired. For the first time in his life he felt an excitement, a whole world was waiting out there, and he knew nothing of what was out there. He wanted to explore. The world of biotechnology beckoned him, and he was restless, unable to contain himself to begin the journey.

Mrs. Tenny suggested that he contact both Stanford and MIT and inform them of the offer he had from Johns Hopkins. Maybe, they will make a counter-offer. Harper dismissed the idea, saying that he preferred to go where they wanted him from the get-go. Tenny couldn't find an argument against that decision. She told him that she was very happy for him and that he would go far no matter where he began his journey.

"Mrs. Tenny, I really want to thank you for your guidance and support. I would not have had this opportunity if you had not pushed me to apply to all these schools. I never imagined...."

"Of course, Curtis, it is my job and really a pleasure to see my students reach for the stars. I love my job, and this time of year is absolutely the best. I see so many wonderful stories, wonderful beginnings. I wish you the best."

Chapter 2:
Stocks Are Smarter Than Humans

Curtis Harper was brilliant. Johns Hopkins was a breeze. He graduated from Johns Hopkins near the top of his class. His research into drugs to lower cardiovascular risk led him to graduate program at University of Southern California and continued post graduate research at Northwestern University. After he earned his Doctorate in Philosophy (Ph.D.), Harper was promptly hired by Novartis, a big pharmaceutical company with its tentacles in hundreds of drug trials. Dr. Harper was pursuing his life's work and passion.

Novartis changed him. He had seen the scientists at Novartis work hard and run long and tedious drug trials, yet the rewards did not come their way. The bulk of the rewards and financial remuneration went to the executives in management and ultimately to some of the largest shareholders.

He had seen a ton of small biotechnology companies running successful drug trials only to be bought up by behemoths like Pfizer, Bristol Myers, and others. And the scientists at these smaller companies walked away with a jackpot when their companies got gobbled up by big pharma. Novartis was also on the lookout for acquisition candidates, searching for smaller companies that seemed to have a potential blockbuster drug in their pipeline.

With his love for lowering cardiovascular risk, he had stumbled upon a Dublin-based company called Amarin. And by chance, he stumbled into a decision to buy Amarin stock. He was impressed by the drug trial data, and he gathered enough courage to go ahead and make a decent enough sized purchase of Amarin shares. It was August of 2018. Amarin was trading around $2.75 a share. Over a period of two weeks, Harper bought $250,000 worth of stock with an average buy price of around $2.5 a share. He had 100,000 shares of Amarin.

As if he had a premonition, the following month Amarin skyrocketed to $19.80 on news that its fish-oil capsule significantly reduced cardiovascular risk. Soon the stock was over $20 a share, and suddenly, Curtis Harper's account was worth over two million dollars.

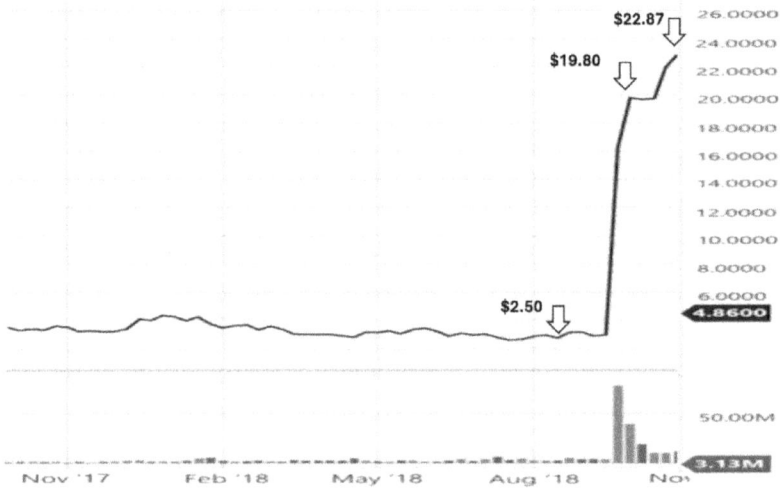

Chart 5.1

Over a period of months, Amarin gyrated between $15 and $22 a share. Weeks turned to months. 2018 turned to 2019. 2019 slowly was going by and before he realized it, Harper was staring at the December 2019 chart of Amarin. Harper strongly believed that he had made the right decision and was fully intending to stick with Amarin shares for what he felt was an impending bonanza. But this had been going on for a bit too long. He did not like the way the stock was acting. But his heart was into the stock, and he felt the stock was going to $100. In his mind, for whatever reason, he had this $100 number imprinted on his brain. He had read some projections for the stock's price in a biotechnology stock market letter and he could not shake it.

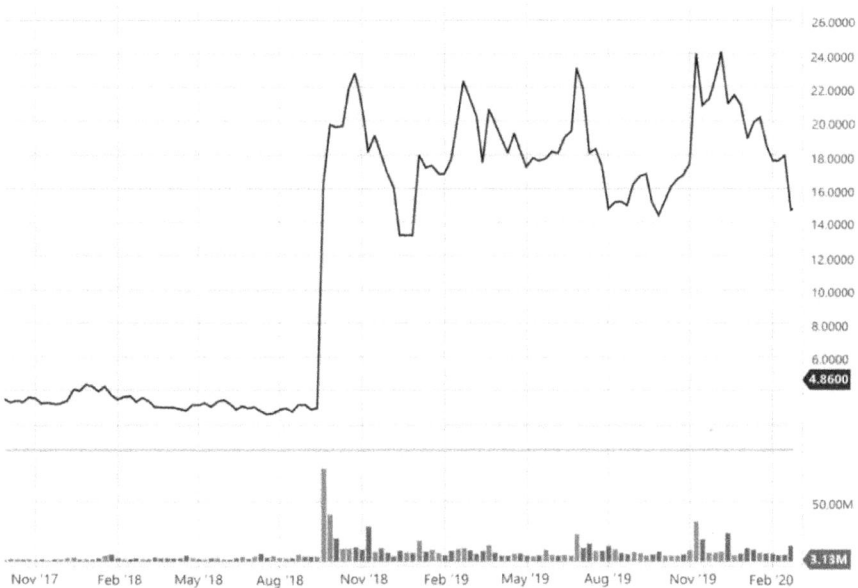

Chart 5.2

Within a matter of weeks, Curtis Harper got hit by a double whammy. The first hit was a lawsuit, a competitor filed a lawsuit against Amarin claiming patent infringement as supposedly the idea of using fish-oil for cardiovascular risk reduction was originally used by the competitor and the lawsuit slammed the stock price. Suddenly the stock dropped to below $10 a share.

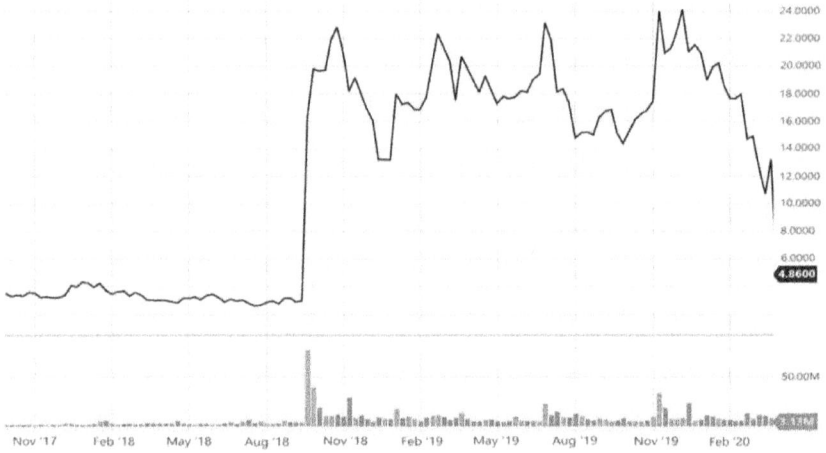

Chart 5.3

And a little while later, unexpectedly, from Harper's viewpoint, the judge agreed with the competitor and decided the case against Amarin. Suddenly Amarin was now trading back in the below $5 range. His almost two million was now worth about half-a-million. He was still up from where he had bought it. And his thinking was that the stock had dropped from $24 to $5 within weeks. And all the bad news about Amarin was now out in the open.

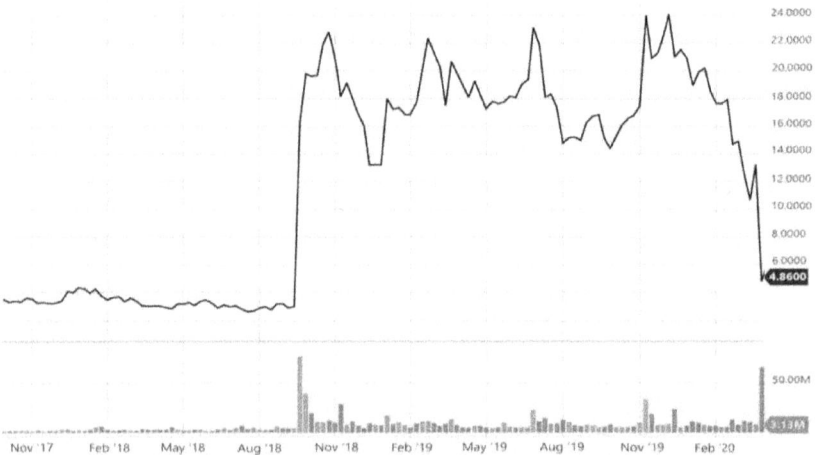

Chart 5.4

The stock can only rebound from this price level. There is no way it can get any lower.

After all, he had a brilliant mind. All his life he had been near the top of his class. At every juncture after school, he continued to be near the top of his profession, interacting with the smartest minds in the world, dealing with complicated and intricate drug trials, case studies, human trials, giving speeches at the top conferences, writing and publishing papers, etc. He was considered a superb brain by his peers.

Curtis Harper had an impression of himself that was probably not accurate, as the stock market has a way of revealing the true self of a human being. But he did not know this. He was holding on to a stock that was not the right stock at the right time. He had failed to see this.

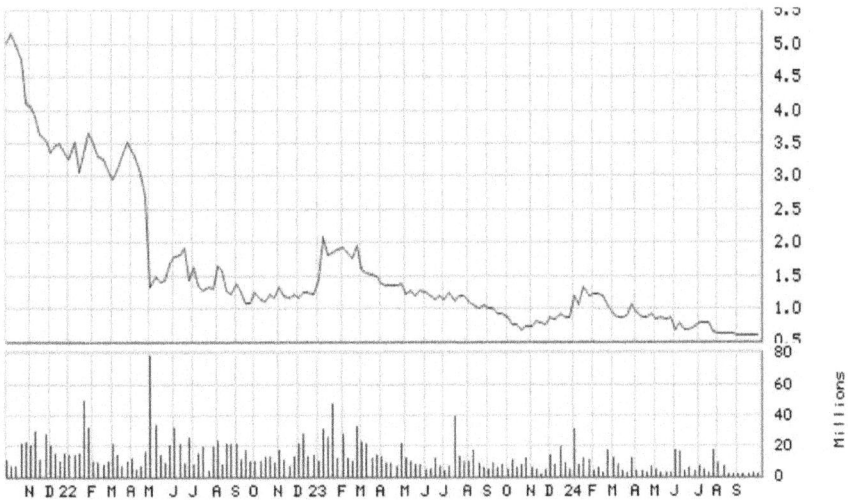

Chart 5.5

Chapter 3:
Being Foolish Is Smarter

While he was in deep despair and worsening mental condition, Curtis Harper reached out to one of his old college classmates and a close friend, Phil Seitz, who was now a research scientist at another biotechnology company called Moderna.

After a few minutes spent with Phil Seitz and his calm demeanor, Curtis walked away feeling a lot better. Phil had given Curtis a name and a phone number, a person to contact, to help him understand the intricacies of dealing with stocks.

That weekend Curtis sat down with his phone in his hand, thinking hard about contacting the name that Phil Seitz had given. *Jamie Blankenship*. Curtis dialed the number, and a gruff voice of an older sounding man answered the phone.

"Hallo! Who is calling me?"

"Good morning, Mr. Blankenship. I was given your number by my old classmate, Phil Seitz. He told me that you could help me understand what I did wrong in my stock operation with a stock called Amarin. I am sorry to come straight to the point, but I am in a deep hole and my mind is really going mad."

"That Phil! He needs to stop giving my name out!"

"Oh? I apologize, Mr. Blankenship if I bothered you. Phil is a dear friend. And he was only trying to help me out."

"No, that's alright. Yeah, you played with Amarin, and didn't get out at the right time. Ok, alright, come over in the afternoon, four o'clock. All I can offer you is coffee, if you want anything else then I suggest you bring it yourself. I will text my address. And call me *Ship*."

Jamie Blankenship lived in a nice neighborhood, in a modest home. But it was the inside that indicated that Blankenship was very successful. From the outside, his home looked like a normal three-bedroom home, as estimated by Curtis Harper. The landscape was classy, simple but classy. But the inside was lavishly furnished, the wall hangings were high-end, a lot more expensive than what Harper had expected. The warmth and the casual atmosphere inside made him immediately at ease.

Blankenship was in his seventies, or even maybe in his eighties. For Curtis it was hard place the exact number on Ship's age. Ship was rather fit for a man his age. And the eyes seemed sharp as he invited Harper to have a seat in the breakfast nook where he had a pot of coffee and a couple of coffee cups.

After a brief exchange about Phil Seitz and how nice a man Phil was, Blankenship asked for a brief background on Harper's trades on Amarin. There was nothing Curtis could extract from the stoic face of Blankenship.

"First, please call me *Ship*. Too long a name. Second, I cannot help you with Amarin, which is water under the bridge and a lost cause. Just get out and forget about it. Use the funds in another prospect. I can offer some guidance on another stock that is just now beginning a move. I would expect this stock to teach us all some lessons, and perhaps offer an opportunity to make some gains."

Harper was immediately excited, but he tried to match the calmness and the stillness he saw in Ship, "That would be much appreciated, Ship. I have realized that I do not know much about how stocks operate. I thought that stocks that had great products and good financials or prospects of financials were good investments. I think Amarin proved me wrong."

"There are no investments in the stock market. There are only plays. It is a game that you play. Some plays make you a winner, others make you a loser. It is also quite common to have more losing plays than winning plays.

The key is to win big in your winning plays and lose small in your losing plays."

"So, what you are saying, Ship, is that my Amarin play was a losing play. But instead of taking a big win, and taking a smaller win on a winning play, I ended up taking a big loss and turned it into a losing play?"

"Curtis, Amarin is not a good example. Use this new stock instead. You will see. Do you follow NFL?"

"Not until the playoffs start. Why?

"Because, Harper, in football you could have fourth-and-out on multiple drives. And you could then follow those losing plays with a bunch of third-down conversions and eventually score a touchdown. Just a game. Stocks. A bunch of quick losing plays with even an occasional long drive and still not being to score, followed by a touchdown. Add to it some windy, rainy days and snow blizzard conditions. The challenges are plenty, opportunities few. Just have to learn to make the right plays."

Ship pulled a chart on his iPad and placed it on the table.

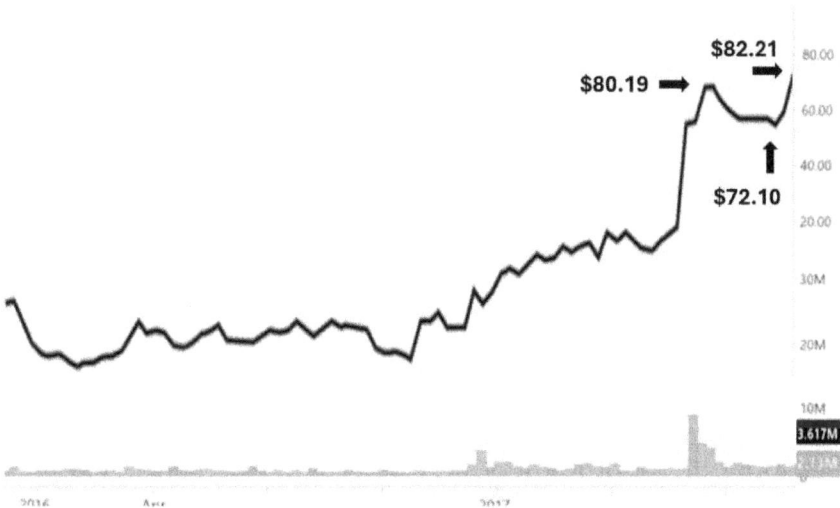

Chart 5.6

"What stock is this? And what am I looking at, Ship?"

"I spoke to Phil Seitz after you called me this morning. He said great things about you. For you to understand, you have to ignore what this company does. It does not matter."

"Huh? You like a stock without knowing what the company makes? How can you do that? Surely, you want to know what it sells and how it makes profits."

"Nope. Not interested. Only interested if its price is rising."

"But how do you know its price is rising, Ship? I mean, it is an $80 stock, how do you know it will go higher?"

"Well, I don't know that it will go up in price in the future. It has gone up in price so far, as you can see from the chart."

"Really, Ship? Do you really want me to believe that such a way of looking at stocks to buy works?"

"Yes, it works, only if you know what do. It stems from a simple fact. A stock that runs from $30 to $200, just does not go up in a straight line It takes two steps forward, one step back. But all the time still moving up, never ever back-tracking below its prior low."

"Ok, then, Ship, please tell me what to do with this stock?"

"It just made a new price high at $82.21, which is higher than the prior high of $80.19. The last low was $72.10. So, a rising stock should not head back below $72.10. Based on this, I would place the following order.

Buy 1000 LOXO @ the market, which would get you filled at $82.21
Sell Stop 1000 LOXO at $60"

"I see what you are suggesting, Ship, to be prepared in advance the amount you would be willing to lose on this play. Now, I am thinking, if I had done this with Amarin, how would I have done it?"

Ship picked up his iPad and entered the ticker AMRN and entered some arrows and annotations and placed it down in front of Curtis Harper. And Harper sat up straight when he saw what Ship had placed in front of him. After a moment, Harper stood up and started pacing back and forth as Ship sat back, cool, and aloof.

Chart 5.7

After what seemed to be several minutes of pacing back-and-forth, Curtis Harper came back and sat down facing Ship and said in a downcast voice, "If I had met you when AMRN was at $24, I would have been sold at the sell-stop you have marked here. At $18. I have 100,000 shares. That is $1,800,000 at $18 a share. But I held on, and held on, and..today the stock is worth sixty cents a share. $0.60! My 100,000 is worth a mere $60,000!"

Ship sat silently. He knew exactly how Curtis felt. A very long time ago, Ship himself had learned his lessons the hard way. That is the only way to learn the lessons, the hard way. That way, you never ever forget the lesson.

The two of them continued talking for a few minutes more when Ship indicated that he had a dinner appointment that he could not miss. He offered Curtis to let him follow along with his trades on LOXO, "If you are interested, I can let you know on my operations on LOXO as and when I make a move. Perhaps, you can catch on a few things so you can recover from the hit on Amarin."

Curtis thanked Blankenship profusely as he headed to the door.

Chapter 4:
Decision Making
Should Be Simple

A couple of weeks later, Curtis got a text from Ship. It was a chart for LOXO.

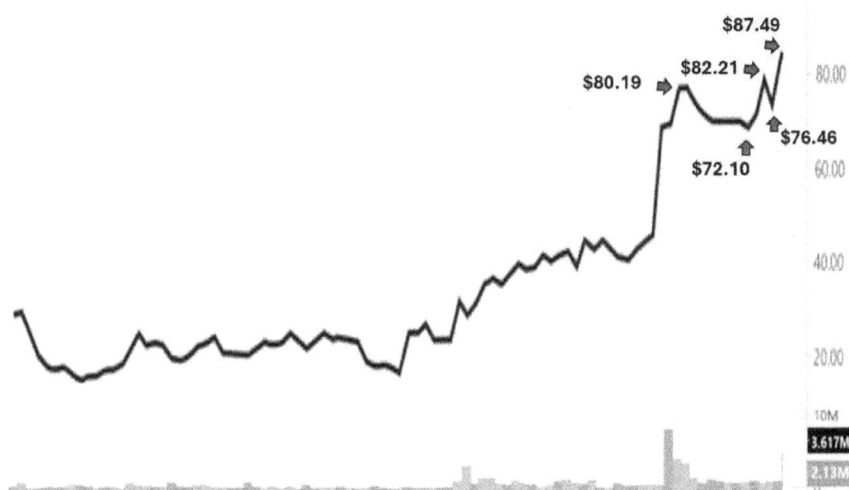

Chart 5.8

Ship: LOXO new high, Buy at 87.49, stop now at 61.18.

Previous buy:

Buy 1000 LOXO @ $82.21

Sell Stop 1000 LOXO at $60

New buy:

Buy 1000 LOXO @ $87.49

Sell Stop 1000 LOXO at $61.18

Total commitment $82,210 + $87,490 = $169.700

Worst case = $169,700 – (2000 x $61.18) = ($47,340)

Harp: Isn't that a lot of risk? Willing to lose $47,340?

Ship: If you can't sleep cut down the amounts by half, still can't sleep? Cut down to 20% of the amount, keep the loss where it won't spoil your sleep.

Harp: Just gun shy after that AMRN trade.

Ship: Have a short memory, previous trade cannot affect your moves on the current trade.

And after yet another couple of weeks, yet another text came from Ship to Curtis Harper's phone.

Ship: LOXO another buy. 3rd buy. Buy 1000 LOXO @ 92.12, sell-stop at $69.48.

3000 LOXO commitment $261,820

Worst-case stop-triggered loss = $261,820 - $208,440 = ($53,380)

If you don't like the loss, reduce the commitment to the point where you don't lose sleep. This is about a 20% drawdown. You adjust your drawdown, and that will dictate the amount committed.

Chart 5.9

Harp: But how many times will you keep buying?

Ship: No way to tell now, I will know when I will know.

After that Ship went silent for a while. Weeks rolled by, and more weeks rolled by. Sixteen weeks later, almost four months had gone by, and Harper waited patiently to hear from Ship. As much as he felt the need to reach to Ship, he controlled himself. Phil Seitz had told him that Ship didn't like it when people bothered him. Harper realized he himself had a lot more patience than he knew. And finally, after all that silence Ship's message popped up.

Ship: Well now, finally, a chance to decide; make a decision. What do you see?

Chart 5.10

Harp: Another new high? I am surprised the low did not hit the stop.

Ship: Yeah, the stop was at $69.48. The low came close, as close as $71.49. But it never hit it.

Harp: How do you figure out the new stop now?

Ship: More by feel, something you learn through experience. What will you do?

Harp: Tough to decide. Without knowing where the stop is, it is tough.

Ship: Suppose the stop is at $83, what will you do?

Harp: I guess I would buy it since the stop has moved up. But how much to buy?

Ship: Buy *1000 LOXO @ $96.83, Stop $83. 4000 LOXO total commitment = $358,650*

4000 LOXO if stopped @ $83 = $332,000, worst-case loss = ($26,650)

Harp, I recommend stop buying. Let it play out now.

Over the next few months, Ship was silent for the most part. Only occasional text messages came from him to Harper. Very sporadic in nature, but always on time with respect to the way the price/volume chart of LOXO seemed to play itself out. The operation was simple enough, with a trailing stop under the latest low pegged by LOXO. The text messages were just one-liners, pretty self-explanatory to Harper.

Chart 5.11

Harper kept a close eye on the process, he had a brilliant mind and all this seemed quite simple to him. But he followed along religiously having learned from his own mistake on Amarin that had cost him a couple of million dollars.

Eventually, the stop that was placed as a trailing stop below the last low of $173.48 was triggered at $156. When Harper ran the numbers, and he wrote down the entire operation's profits and commitment figures, he saw this:

4000 LOXO total commitment = $358, 650

4000 LOXO sold @ $156, received = $624,000

Profit realized = $265,350

Having now seen the profits, suddenly Harper was glad he himself had placed these exact same original amounts in commitments on the LOXO operation. It had escaped him that he had questioned the risk that Ship had recommended in the early positions. A perfectly common human behavior when it comes to money. In real-time, there are all kinds of questions and skepticism. After the fact, should the outcome turn out to be favorable, suddenly the wish becomes that an aggressive commitment should have been made, instead of the skepticism.

Harper had thought that it was the end of LOXO's run and had not paid any attention to the stock after being sold out of his commitments. Then out of the blue, Ship messaged him if he was willing to place all his profits from LOXO back into LOXO for potentially one final play.

Harper was surprised by the text from Ship and asked him what the play was. Ship sent him the chart for LOXO. The chart was annotated. It took Harper less than a minute to make up his mind and he jumped on the play.

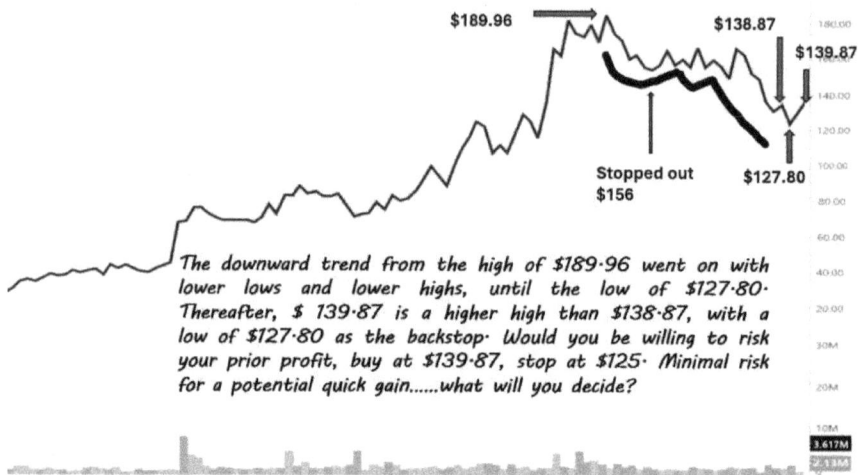

Chart 5.12

Harper had $265,000 in profit from his LOXO operation. He immediately ran some numbers on his calculator.

265,000/139.87 = 1894, buy 1900 LOXO at $139.87

Stop at $125, worst-case scenario, 1900 (139.87 – 125) = $28,253 loss, which I am willing to give back to LOXO, to follow Ship's strategy.

The following Monday morning Curtis Harper was stunned. His trading app was flashing a notification with bright exclamation mark, and a subtext that said, "*Breaking news on LOXO, Click to read.*" Nervously he clicked.

LOXO has agreed to an acquisition by Eli Lilly for cash valued at nearly $8 billion or $234/share of LOXO……

Harper's 1900 shares in LOXO were now worth $444,600, all of it was his profit from the entire LOXO play. Harper wondered about how Ship knew of the play. How did Ship know this inside news? It seemed like this purchase of LOXO by Lilly was known only to the insiders, but somehow Ship had played the game as an insider from the outside.

Chart 5.13

Curtis Harper was in the biotechnology business and he himself had no idea of the pending LOXO and Eli Lilly deal. But the stock itself had been flashing this message for months. The message was only visible to those that had developed the skill of observing. But just observing was not enough. How did one interpret the things that one observed? And how did one act on the things on interpreted?

Curtis was pacing back and forth for a while. He had to find a way to learn the things that Ship knew. That knowledge was priceless.

Harp: Ship, that was a wonderful play and a great learning experience. How do I go about learning the skills?

Ship: You just have to go through the journey yourself, my friend, no substitute for it – that's the only way of learning. By actually doing it yourself.

Case Study #6
It Is Smart To Be The Perfect Fool

Chapter 1:
The Strange Fool

The Fool had become an urban legend at the local coffee shop. Ever since the originally named, *The Corner Coffee Shop,* had changed its name to *The Perfect Coffee, You Fool,* the fool had found it hard to go back to that coffee shop no matter how much he missed their excellent freshly brewed coffee. This was a mid-sized North Atlantic coastal city, small enough to feel neighborly, yet large enough to have a big-city feel.

The Fool prized his privacy, which was just his mentality. And in many ways, it was the reclusive and rather eccentric behavior that had made him learn all the lessons he had learned in the stock market. To the outside world he was just an old non-descript man who seemed and acted odd. He clearly had rather odd ways of social interaction. Whether it was a trait he was born with and couldn't overcome, or it was a learned behavior, no one could tell. There was also a possibility that it was a front he put on to avoid social contact.

It was his odd behavior, strange mannerisms, and weird way of communicating that had earned him the name *The Fool.* He couldn't remember, nor did he care, how and where that name first stuck to him. It had been a long time ago and now he was in his seventies, and he had lost sense of time.

He had to find a new and a different coffee shop to fulfill his need for his Friday afternoon coffee. This was a strange habit among the many he had. He had to have his coffee on Fridays, usually wandering into his favorite coffee shop at 3:30 pm. One could set one's watch by the punctuality with which he walked in. Every Friday afternoon at 3:30 pm on the dot. No one knew why only on Fridays, nor did anyone know as to why exactly at 3:30 pm. He would stay till 4:00 pm, exactly thirty minutes, again very strictly sticking to the time. Exactly thirty minutes. He would leave at 4:00 pm on the dot whether he had finished his coffee or not. At 4:00 pm, time took precedence over coffee. He had to get up and leave at 4:00 pm no matter what, no matter who wanted to talk to him or not.

It was one such Friday afternoon when *The Fool* was lost in his own thoughts and sipping on his coffee, when he overhead the woman sitting at a table nearby speaking on the phone. Something she said on the phone perked up his ears. He stopped drinking his coffee and sat still, trying to pay close attention to the words she was saying.

"But Mom! Dad has already had a second and a third opinion. There are not very many options for prostate cancer."

The Fool slowly turned around as if he was looking for the waitress and briefly scanned the room while his eyes quickly took in the visual of the woman who was speaking on her phone to her mother. He estimated she was probably in her forties, well dressed, with a businesswoman look about her. Probably a lawyer or some kind of an executive, he thought.

The Fool pulled out a few dollars and placed them on the check that always accompanied his coffee. He pulled out a piece of paper and a pen from his shirt pocket and wrote a small note. Then he got up and started walking towards the door to head out of the coffee shop. On his way towards the door, he had to pass the lady talking to her mom on the phone.

For a brief moment as he was close to her table his eyes met hers, and his eyes immediately averted hers. And he placed the note he had written on her table and walked out. The businesswoman stared at the note for a moment and turned around to look for the man who left that note for her. But he had already left the coffee shop.

She looked at the note in front of her. She picked it up and opened the note to see what it said.

Try ECYT.

Confused, she called the waitress over. She handed the note to the waitress and asked if it made any sense. The waitress was equally confused and shook her head.

The businesswoman said, "There was this man sitting over there and as he walked his way out he dropped this note on my table. Strange."

The waitress muttered, "He comes here every Friday around this time. If you want to talk to him, maybe you can come back next week?"

Chapter 2:
What Is ECYT?

Though every cell in her brain told her not do it, the businesswoman just could not help herself. She walked into the coffee shop on the following Friday afternoon hoping to catch the man who had dropped her the note. She scanned the coffee shop and there he was, sitting at a corner table all by himself drinking his coffee.

She walked over to him, without asking firmly planted herself across from him and held out her hand to shake his hand, "Tracy Abbott. How are you?"

The man seemed confused for a moment. He shook her hand and nodded, "Yes, Tracy Abbott. How are you?"

"You left this note for me last week. And you ran away before I could talk to you. I am curious, what does this note mean?"

"What does this note mean? What does this note mean? It means try ECYT."

"Yes, of course, I can read, mister. But what does this mean?"

"ECYT. She is a good one for prostate cancer,"

Tracy was taken aback. Is this a new drug or some kind of cure for prostate cancer? In desperation, she asked for information about himself. Who was he? What did he know about prostate cancer? Was this a cure for prostate cancer? The barrage of questions came out fast and furious. She was excited and did not notice the nervousness with which the man was staring at her without a word.

The manager of the coffee shop walked up to her. She looked up at him.

"Miss, I am Oliver. I own this coffee shop. Is everything ok?"

"Hello Oliver. I am Tracy. Yes, everything is ok. Why do you ask?"

"This here is my friend and a loyal patron who is a regular customer of our coffee shop. He likes his privacy and likes to be left alone. I saw you being a bit excited, and it looked to me from where I was standing that you were almost yelling at my friend here. He is a sensitive man, a kind man, one who does not take loud noises and people yelling very well. I just want to make sure that he is being treated well."

"Oh, I apologize. I might have come across as being aggressive. But last week he left me a note and I wanted to know what the note meant. See here, he left this note that says *Try ECYT*. What does that mean? I ask just asking him to explain the meaning, that's all."

Oliver turned to *The Fool*, "Should I ask Tracy here to leave you alone?"

The Fool nodded. Oliver escorted Tracy over to a different table, away from *The Fool*. As Tracy sat down, Oliver said, "Tracy, I suggest you leave him alone unless he opens the door to a conversation. My friend over there has issues with social interaction and likes to be left alone. With regard to this note, I would surmise this is a stock. Look up its ticker symbol, ECYT. My man, *The Fool*, as we all call him around here, is a stock market genius of sorts. He knows things others don't. This might turn out to be your lucky day."

That evening Tracy was on the internet spending a lot of time checking out ECYT. It turned out that ECYT was a ticker symbol for a small biotechnology company focused on developing a drug for prostate cancer. It was developing a drug that found a way to attack only cancerous cells without affecting healthy cells. The drug seemed very promising.

She then looked up its stock chart. Just to see what had been happening with the stock price. The stock price had quadrupled recently based on the news of results of some drug trial. *This is good. That is a good sign.*

Whatever other information Tracy could glean from the internet seemed to point to positive outcomes for test trial patients. She immediately called her mom and discussed about making an appointment with another specialist for her father's prostate cancer and see if Endocyte's drugs were worth it.

A few months passed by. And Tracy Abbott lost her father to prostate cancer. A few weeks later, without any forethought, she found herself walking into the coffee shop where she had met *The Fool* months ago. It was a Friday afternoon around 3;30 pm. She was deep in thought, sipping her coffee and didn't even notice *The Fool* walking in. Tracy was so lost in her thoughts that she had not paid attention to *The Fool* making himself comfortable across from her at her table.

It was only when he pulled out a piece of paper and wrote a note and handed it to her that she realized what had just happened. She was too confused to do anything but to pick up the note and read it.

Buy ECYT today!

"What? You are suggesting I buy the stock of Endocyte today?

The Fool was surprised by Tracy's reaction and seemed just echo her words, "You are suggesting I buy the stock of Endocyte today? Are you?"

Tracy Abbot pulled out her phone and checked its stock chart. It seemed to be at a multi-year price high. She turned to *The Fool* and said, "I don't know about buying that stock. It is too expensive. It has risen four-fold in the past year alone. There is not a chance that it goes any higher."

The Fool stood up, and before he walked away, he said, "Make the right decision. Just buy a small amount then. What is the worst thing that can happen? Place a stop at $3.75 and calculate the amount you want to risk. So simple." Tracy noticed that *The Fool* sounded almost normal just then. *Was he putting on an act to fool the people around him? What if he really was a genius masquerading as The Fool?*

At that point she found herself calling in a buy order for two thousand shares of Endoctye. When she hung up after talking to her broker, she immediately started having buyer's remorse. She had bought based purely on her gut feel of what she felt when *The Fool* spoke about decision-making. Tracy had learned to rely on her gut instinct whenever she tried her cases. Her legal career had taken off once she had figured out that her instincts were her best friend.

As a typical lawyer would, she wrote down her numbers,

Bought 2,000 ECYT @ 6.5 Stop $3.75 GTC

Spent $13,000.

Total Commitment = $13,000

Worst-Case Scenario = ($5,500)

Tracy Abbott didn't seem to care that as a percentage of her commitment, the worst-case scenario was a significant drawdown. In some respects, she seemed to have the mental outlook of a true speculator. The prospect of a loss did not deter her. A trait she had developed a long time ago in her legal profession. Being scared of a potential loss would end up in a self-fulfilling prophecy, her father, another lawyer of some repute, had taught her. She would repeat his words often. *Play the game with confidence, my dear.*

Unknown to her at that time, *The Fool* had the chart for ECYT embedded in his brain. He had been following it for months, for over seven months in fact. In its price and volume action, he had seen things he recognized immediately as a potential big bang stock. He patiently waited for the right behavior by the stock. And he saw it when the stock seemed to want to close above the $6.00 price. And that was the day he had dropped the hint to Tracy to buy the stock. To his eyes the message from the chart was unmistakable. The test was going to be to see whether one could play it the right way. His own motto, same as that of Tracy's father, but applied to stock market operations was, *Play the Game The Right Way.*

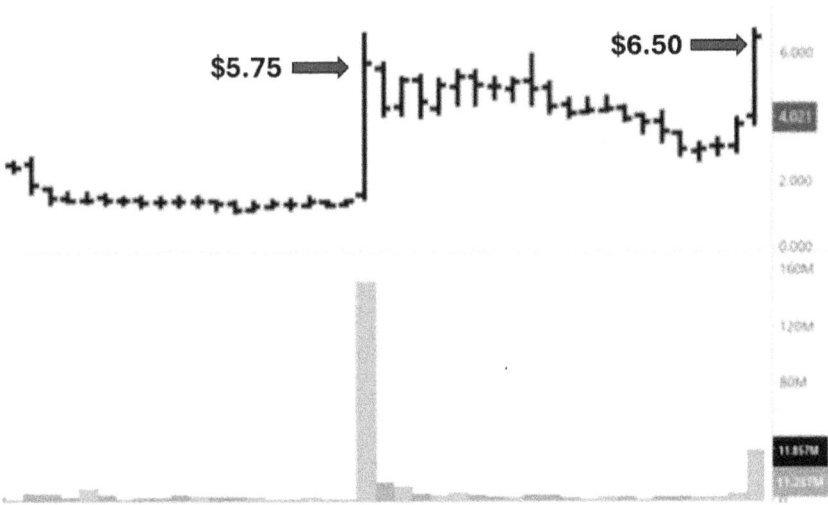

Chart 6.1

A few weeks later, on yet another Friday, Tracy sauntered into the coffee shop looking for *The Fool*. He was sitting at his usual spot, with his usual cup of coffee with his usual look on his face. A look of detachment and confusion at the same time. Tracy made herself comfortable across from him at his table. And smiled.

"I know that this whole fool thing is an act. You are a genius, probably stemming from the years of experience, your own experience of trading, winning, and losing and winning big."

The Fool nodded, smiled back, and said, "Yes, it is an act. A genius. A big win, a big win."

"Cut it out, no need to carry on the charade. By the way, that was a good call on Endocyte. How did you know?"

The Fool looked as if he did not hear Tracy. He slowly reached into his pocket and pulled a small notebook. He tore a blank sheet out of the notebook. And started drawing a chart. While he was drawing, never looking up to meet Tracy's eyes, he said, "Cut out the charade. How did you know about Endocyte? Because she will make a new high today. You buy more. Decide properly. Check your risk. Buy more today, before the market closes in a few minutes."

He placed the chart he had drawn in front of Tracy. Still without meeting Tracy's eyes, *The Fool* got up and left. Tracy was left sitting there, staring down at the chart.

Chart 6.2

Tracy immediately pulled her phone out of her purse and called her broker.

"Buy 10,000 ECYT at market, once filled sell-stop 12,000 ECYT at $8.99." She was told that she got filled at $10.89/share. She ran her numbers.

Bought 10,000 ECYT @ 10.89 Stop $8.99 GTC

Spent $108,900.

Total Commitment = $13,000 + $108.900 = $121,900

Worst-Case Scenario = $121,900 – (12,000 x $8.99) = ($14,020)

The speculator's blood in her veins couldn't be denied. As her commitment grew larger, her risk as a percentage of the commitment fell. Again, her father's words came to her mind. *A risk is a risk only if you don't know what you are doing.*

It had been some time since her father had lost his battle with prostate cancer. And here was a company, Endocyte, that seemed to have developed a drug that looked promising for prostate cancer patients. What else could be the reason for the stock price run-up? Clearly, someone with deep pockets was betting on the stock. She intended to bring this up with *The Fool* the following Friday.

Chapter 3:
A Gambler Versus A Speculator

Tracy was early that Friday. She got there a good half-an-hour before *The Fool's* usual arrival time. She found Oliver at the cash register and asked him if he had a few minutes to talk. Oliver obliged and walked with her to her table and sat down across from Tracy.

"How can I help you?"

"Oliver, I appreciate you taking the time to talk to me. I am interested in knowing more about *The Fool*. You were right. He is a really sharp guy. I think he is putting on a front. This fool thing is a front, a façade."

"You think so? I don't know. I have known him for a while now. I came to know of him through a friend who owns another coffee shop across town. *The Fool* used to hang out at his coffee shop until one day too many people wanted a piece of him, especially when they found out about his gift for stock picking."

"But his front is a façade I feel. There is no way someone so sharp is not able to communicate properly. I am a financial lawyer, and I have seen some brilliant guys. *The Fool* is a brilliant guy."

"I think you are jaded, Tracy, given your lawyer background and stuff. He is as real as they come. Really nice guy too. Just awkward with people, that's all. I know it hard to imagine that a guy so gifted in one area is so lacking in another. But such is life."

"I get the sense you like *The Fool*."

"What is there not to like? He is quiet, keeps to himself. Gives me no trouble. He enjoys his coffee, pays his check and leaves. I think he likes that I keep an eye on him, you know, keep folks away from him."

"Would you keep me away from him too? What if I really wanted to talk to him? Real talk, no drama, no games."

"Tracy, I will only stop you if *The Fool* wants me to stop you. It is up to him. It depends on the vibe I get when I see the two of you together."

Oliver went back to his position at the cash register. Just then *The Fool* walked in and sat at his usual table. Tracy gave Oliver a nod and walked over to *The Fool* and sat at his table, across from him.

"Hey! How are you doing today?" Tracy flashed a smile at *The Fool*.

There was no perceptible reaction on *The Fool's* face. He just nodded and repeated the same words, "Hey! How are you doing today?"

"I was talking to Oliver, and I told him that I thought this whole thing is an act. You know, you being *The Fool* and all. You are very clever. You think you act like a fool and people will leave you alone. Yet, you pick and choose who and when you will approach. I mean, there I was, minding my own business and you could have just walked by. Yet, you just had to drop me a note about Endocyte. That tells me, that you wanted to be involved in my business."

"Yes, be in involved in my business. Endocyte is my business. Minding my own business."

Tracy was silent for a moment. Stirring her coffee. Then she pulled out her own notebook and wrote a note and handed it to *The Fool*. He couldn't wait, he grabbed the note and looked at it impatiently. For someone so deliberate, the impatience stood out to Tracy as she sat there watching intently. He looked at the note that read:

First buy:

Bought 2,000 ECYT @ 6.5 Stop $3.75 GTC

Spent $13,000.

Second buy:

Bought 10,000 ECYT @ 10.89 Stop $8.99 GTC

Spent $108,900.

All Total:

Total Commitment = $13,000 + $108,900 = $121,900

Worst-Case Scenario = $121.900 – (12,000 x $8.89) = ($14,020)

It was Tracy's position placement on ECYT.

"Don't buy any more. Move your stops up as the price makes a higher low."

The words came out authoritatively and Tracy took note and nodded.

Now it was *The Fool's* turn to drop a note. He pulled out a pen, flipped over the note that Tracy had handed to him. And drew a chart.

"Be a speculator, not a gambler," said *The Fool.*

"What do you mean?" asked Tracy.

$10.89 →

Keep
Raising
Your
Stop

Chart 6.3

"If she goes up, do not buy more. And keep trailing the rising low with your stop."

And then *The Fool*, for the first time, met Tracy's gaze eye-to-eye. It lasted a couple of seconds at most, but Tracy felt she had cracked open a door and perhaps there was an opportunity to continue to communicate with *The Fool.*

But, as the weeks and the months went by, Tracy kept coming to the coffee shop in the hopes of finding *The Fool* and he was nowhere to be found. She approached Oliver and asked if he had seen *The Fool.* Oliver had not either. It was with some amount of sadness that the realization came to her that was the last time she would ever see him and *The Fool* was forever out of her life. *The Fool* had stopped coming to that particular coffee shop.

Perhaps he found another coffee shop, away from people who would bother him with human contact, bother him with the human tendency to communicate. It turned out that he was not much of a people person, exactly as Oliver had informed Tracy. For a moment, a thought occurred to Tracy, that perhaps she could stop by some of the other coffee shops in town and look for him. Soon she realized the futility of the exercise, there were just so many coffee shops in town. Moreover, he could have left town for all she knew. And she pushed that thought aside.

She followed the steps as recommended by *The Fool.* She had understood that there was a method to his madness, he had seen things very few had. One day, she remembered it was a Monday, Tracy woke to the news that Endocyte had been bought up by Novartis, a big pharma company. Nervously she opened her phone app to her trading account.

Novartis had agreed to purchase Endocyte for \$24/share. She looked at her account's value and stared at the number flashing back at her. She ran her numbers, and slowly with equal amount of amazement and excitement, with a shaking hand that she tried hard to control as she jotted down the entire trade.

First buy:

Bought 2,000 ECYT @ 6.5 Stop \$3.75 GTC

Spent \$13,000.

Second buy:

Bought 10,000 ECYT @ 10.89 Stop \$8.99 GTC

Spent \$108,900

All Total:

Total Commitment = \$13,000 + \$108.900 = \$121,900

Sold out:

12,000 ECYT @ $24 = $288,000

12,000 ECYT Cost = $121,900

Profit = $166,100

She had to exert zero effort, and the amount of work she had to do to make this profit was also zilch. It had all started with a phone call she was having with her mother that *The Fool* had overheard, a passing mention of prostate cancer. And *The Fool* had entered her life with a note dropped on her table. And he had just as casually walked out of her life, with another note on her table.

And she had made a profit of $166,100 via this note passing exercise. She smiled, reminiscing about the note passing from elementary school, none of those notes amounted to anything. She wished she had found a way to spend more time with *The Fool*.

Tracy then clicked on the newsfeed about the Endocyte and Novartis deal and it read:

BREAKING NEWS: Today's premarket action focuses on a surprising deal that Novartis made by agreeing to purchase Endocyte for $2.1 billion in cash or $24/share. Just a few months ago, Endocyte shares were trading at $1.17/share and ... ...

Tracy was not much interested in the details of the deal. It did not concern her. Her reward had already been received. She was now seeking to find other similar opportunities in the market. She clicked on her charting program and printed out a chart of Endocyte and marked in the uptrend.

Chart 6.4

Case Study #7
Do Not Be Blind To
The Observation

Chapter 1:
An Exercise In Observation

One day while you were minding your own business, you got a phone call. At first you ignored the call. It said it is a private number on the caller ID, and you were not in the habit of answering calls from strangers. After a few rings, the call ended. But a few seconds later, your phone rang again. Same screen showed on the caller ID, it said *Private Number*.

For some reason you decided to pick up the phone.

"Hello."

"Hello, I am Sonia. I am trying to Renata Wierink, she helps me because I am blind."

"Hello Sonia. I am sorry you have the wrong number, there is no Renata at his number. This my number, I have had it for years."

"I see. I see. I am sorry. I am sorry to bother you, but I cannot see, and I need help with looking at stock charts. Would you be kind enough to take a look at a chart on your computer for me? I can guide you as to what to look for."

You were intrigued. Being the stock market student that you are, you offered to help Sonia, "Ok Sonia. I will be happy to help you. I am a stock market enthusiast myself. So, this might turn out to be fun."

Sonia seemed quite happy, "Ok, thank you! I really appreciate this. I am specially looking for stocks that made a new 52-week high this last week. But it is the stock's charts that I am interested in."

You thought for a moment, and said, "I don't think that is a problem. I use a charting service that lists the stocks that made 52-week new highs as well as their charts. What kind of charts are you looking for?"

"Just simple price/volume charts. You can choose whether you wish to use bar charts, OHLC, or line charts as long as both price and volume are shown it doesn't really matter to me."

You are most familiar with line charts, and you decided to go with line charts. And you were flipping through charts of stocks that made a new 52-week high that week and you briefly described each chart to Sonia. She kept passing one stock after another, saying, "Ok, that was not so interesting, let's pass and go to the next one."

Until eventually you came to the chart shown below. And when you described the chart to her, she got a little animated. "This one looks good, very good! Describe once again exactly what are you seeing?"

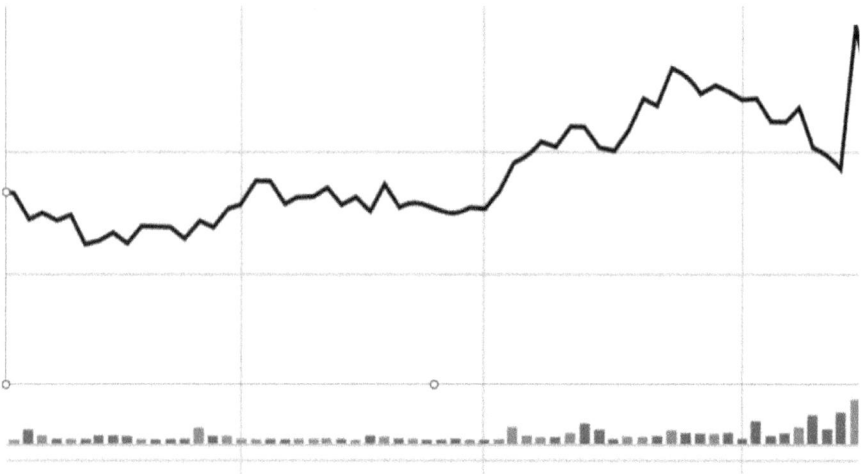

Chart 7.1

"What specifically am I looking for?"

Sonia thought for a moment and said, "Is the volume this week, as it makes a new 52-week high, the highest volume in the past year or so? Also, do you have an ability to annotate and mark specific points if I offer you some guidance?"

"Yes, Sonia, this week was the highest weekly volume as it made a new high. And, yes, I can annotate, mark, and draw anything with my charting service on this chart. What would you like me to draw? Or mark in?"

"This is going to be a bit difficult for me to try and explain, but let's do it step-by-step. First, mark in the new high price. Then mark in the prior high price. Using the prior high price as the tip, draw a horizontal line through the tip of the prior high price. As you draw this, and mark these in, please tell me what you are doing so I can picture it in my head."

"Ok, Sonia, let me first mark the new high price, which is $16.07. The prior high price was $13.98. And let me draw the horizontal line passing through the point marked as $13.98."

Sonia exclaimed, "That was perfect! Now I can picture $16.07 in my head, and relative to $16.07, I can imagine $13.98 as the prior lower high. Now, what was the low pegged between the prices $13.98 and $16.07?"

"It was $9.30."

Sonia shot back immediately, "How long did it take to go from $9.30 to $16.07?"

When you looked at the chart you were surprised and said, "Just one week, and it zoomed from $9.30 to $16.07 in just one week!"

Sonia asked, "Ok, a few more questions to get the image of the chart seared in my head. How many weeks did it take from $13.98 to $9.07 to $16.07?"

You looked at the chart and counted the number of volume bars and you answered, "I think thirteen weeks."

Sonia instructed further, "Mark in the low prior to $13.98. And then go back a step and mark in the low before that low. Oh, also, do not forget to circle the volume for this week to indicate that this week was the highest volume in the past year or so."

You followed her instructions and the chart that is in front of you looked like this.

Chart 7.2

Sonia took a moment, as if to visualize the chart in her head. Then she said, "Now look for a four-year chart, weekly chart, for this stock and tell me what you see."

The chart that shows up looks like this.

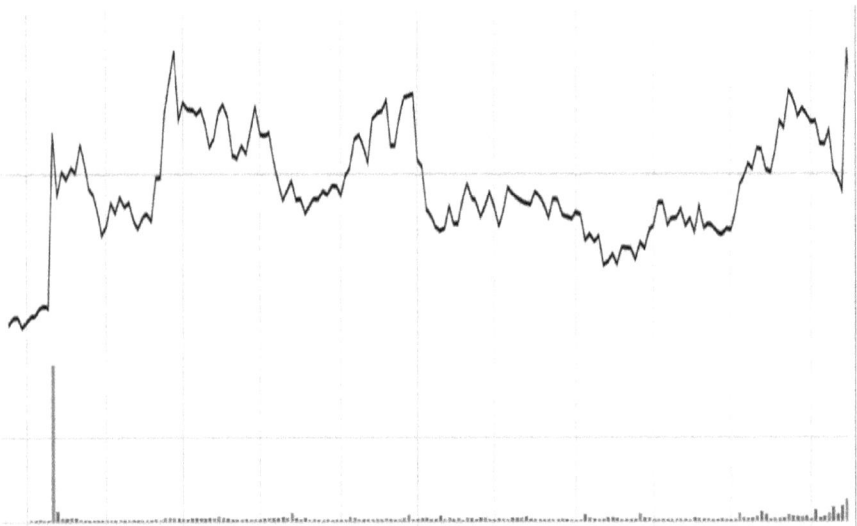

Chart 7.3

Sonia continues, "Ok, now I need you to mark in a few things. On this chart mark the $16.07 price, and circle that week's volume first as the baseline. Next, if there was a prior high higher than $16.07, mark it. If not, then mark the closest prior high to $16.07. Then check for the volume bars. Was there a week with a higher volume than the week you already previously had circled in the prior chart? Circle that volume bar, the one with the higher volume than the one already circled."

Sonia waited until you were done, and once you had finished all the marking in, she asked you to give her more information on the chart in front of you.

"Ok. Now, was there a prior high that was higher than $16.07? Was there a volume bar higher than the volume bar at $16.07? If so, what was the high for that higher volume week? Mark all of these in and let us find out what the chart says."

You looked at your chart and it looked like this.

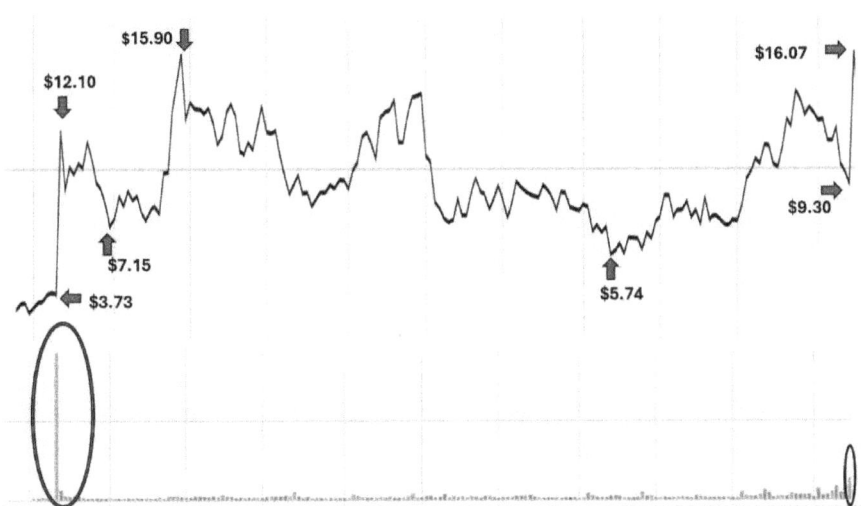

Chart 7.4

You responded, "No, $16.07 was the highest high in the past four years. The prior high was $15.90, just barely lower than the latest high of $16.07.

With regards to volume, there was only one prior week when the volume was higher than the volume bar at $16.07. It was way back in June of 2020. The high of that highest volume week was $12.10. The high of $15.90 was made after that highest volume week at $12.10."

Sonia sat for a moment. Then asked, "Did you mark in the lows between the highs? If not, go ahead and mark the lows in between the highs."

You answered, with some amount of self-pride, "Yeah, already did that. The low between $12.10 and $15.90 was $7.15. And the low between the highs at $15.90 and $16.07 was $5.74."

Sonia asked if you knew how to draw trend curves. You nodded and went ahead and drew them on the chart, and suddenly the chart looked like a picture that told a story. Perhaps it was not clear to you, but you realized that it seemed to project a picture in Sonia's mind.

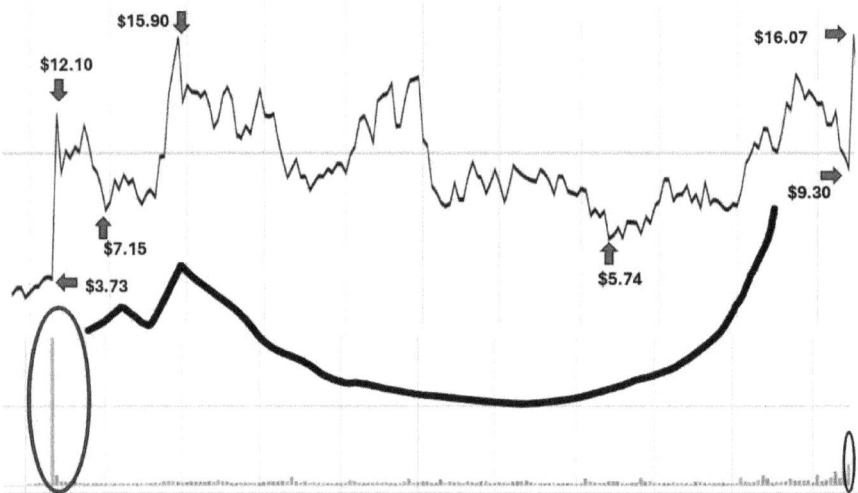

Chart 7.5

Sonia said, "Tell me if I am right. But in my mind, I can picture the chart thus. There was a volume explosion at $12.10. Then a reaction low pegged at $7.15. And then a new high, a high higher than $12.10 was pegged at

$15.90. Then another reaction to $5.74. The low at $5.74 is lower than the prior low of $7.15, negating what would seem like the beginning of an uptrend. And then a new higher high at $16.07, that was higher than the prior high at $15.90. Does that sound about right?"

You were stunned that a blind woman could picture the chart so well. You added, "Wow, that was on point! Only thing that I would like to mention is that the stock went from a low $3.73 to $12.10 on that heaviest volume week in just one week. And again, from the low at $9.30 to the new high at $16.07 again in just one week."

"Ok, that is good to know, yes, that is good to know. Ok, so now I have a request. We have to reconnect every Friday afternoon from now on. And we are going to watch this stock. It looks good, and it is demanding that we watch it closely. And we should listen to this stock's demand that it wants us to watch it. I wonder if I should call you next Friday and if you would be willing to do this for me. I can compensate for your time and work quite handsomely."

You were flabbergasted and replied, "Of course, Sonia, I rather enjoyed this exercise. I am learning so much, so please feel free to call me any time. Honestly, there is no need to pay me, I want to do this because I think what I will learn is worth many fold what you wish to pay me."

Thus began the weekly phone calls between Sonia and you. Now you could not wait for Fridays to come along. Waiting out the weekdays, one by one, was now much harder. When you look forward to an event or an occasion, somehow it seems like time stands still and it seems to take a long time to arrive. The next four Fridays passed by without much fanfare or any memorable events with the stock that you and Sonia were watching.

It was the fifth week, the fifth Friday since Sonia's first wrongly dialed call to you, that the stock showed a new sign of life. And the chart that you were drawing and marking for Sonia changed.

When Sonia called, you were already a step ahead and said, "Hey Sonia, finally, the stock made a new high again this week. We still have a few minutes until market close, but it looks to be closing above the $19 price mark!"

Sonia said, "Ok, that is good, but we must wait till the close. Let's make sure it is new closing high. In the meantime, can you check what the prior low was? I refer to the low between today's price and the prior high price of $16.07. There is a low pegged between these two prices. Where was that low pegged? Was it higher than its prior low that I remember as being $9.30?"

By the time you opened your laptop and brought the chart up, the market had closed. And you finished up the additional tasks that Sonia had given, as to where to mark in the prices. And you came up with the chart that looked like this one below. Sonia asked you to cut and paste the latest few weeks of action in an insert within the long-term chart.

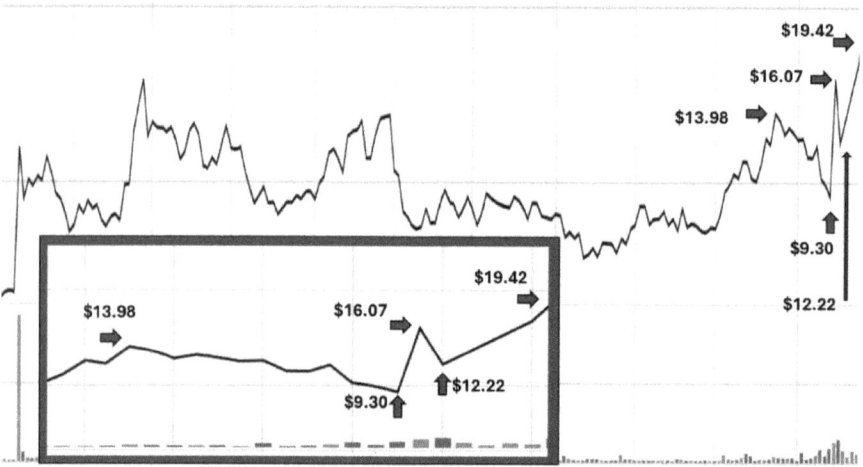

Chart 7.6

Sonia then asked you to draw the trending curves to indicate and illustrate the latest few weeks of price movements that seemed like a new uptrend. You followed her instructions and came with a not-so-good-looking picture as shown below.

Chart 7.7

The main thing was, though, that you noticed the rising trend of the price movements. You noticed that from $13.98 to $16.07 to $19.42, the highs kept going higher. And from $9.30 to $12.22 the corresponding lows were also trending higher.

Sonia immediately said with some firmness in her voice, "There will be a reaction low to the new high at $19.42. As long as that low remains above $12.22, it would be a good sign. And should a new higher high come about after the new higher low, a high higher than $19.42, we will buy this stock!"

There was a finality to her voice that you detected and wondered at the steely determination in her statement. What made her say such a thing? Why so much conviction? All the questions you wanted to ask but could not without sounding too nosy. You thought to yourself to wait it out and see what happens.

Chapter 2:
Let There Be Action

Four weeks later the action began. It was the usual phone call from Sonia, by now it was coming in like clockwork. Every Friday afternoon a few minutes before the market closed. This Friday was no different, except there was a bit of urgency in Sonia's voice.

"Hi Sonia, how are you? That stock seems to be making a new high today."

"Yeah, I think it will offer a buy today. We need to hurry because I must call my broker before the market closes to place my trade. Let us just focus on the chart from the moment it made the high at $13.98. Do you remember that price? It was a high prior to the high at $16.07."

You replied, "Yes, yes, of course. I remember."

"Perfect. We have to show each new high and each new low all the way to the present, including today's new high. And then we need to show the trending curve to reinforce in our minds that we are dealing with an up-trending stock. Let me know when you have the chart completed with the annotations and the mark-ins."

You then spent a few minutes and prepared the chart, which looks like the one below.

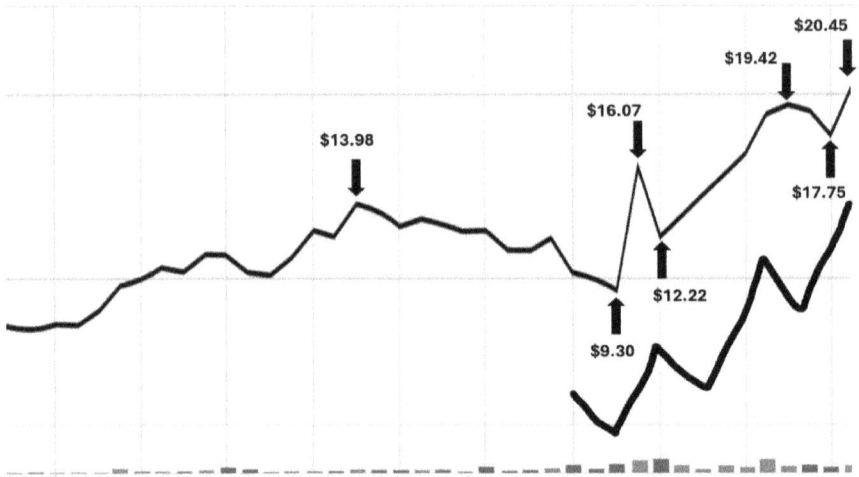

Chart 7.8

"I need you to focus on only two prices on the chart. The latest new high. And the previous low just before this new high. Please give me those two figures so I memorize the numbers."

You looked at the chart you prepared and said, "The new high is at $20.45. And the prior low is at $17.75."

Sonia immediately asked you to run some numbers and she said, "Ok, my friend, I have to now call my broker and place my trade. You have been of utmost help."

Before she hung up the phone you wanted to know the details of her trade. You requested it as a way to learn to trade. Sonia obliged. You wrote down her trade as the phone call ended. After the call ended, you logged into your own trading account and placed your own trade. Since Sonia had suggested that every trade needs to be written down in a journal, you opened a small notebook that you decided to use as your *Journal Of Trade Secrets.*

Buy 200 ALPN at $20.45 Sell-stop $15.95 GTC

Commitment = 200 x $20.45 = $4,090

Worst case I get stopped out, 200 x $15.95 = $3,190

I have resigned myself to lose = $900

This was the first time in your life you ever entered your trade into a notebook. It seemed so much a habit of an older generation.

A couple of Fridays later, the stock made yet another new high, and according to Sonia it was an action Friday. After the usual routine of your chart mark-ins and annotations, she said, "Ok, time for me to call my broker for my next trade."

Yet again Sonia was forthcoming with her suggestions when you asked her about what the recommended amount should be that you committed to the trade.

Chart 7.9

Buy 100 ALPN at $25.12 Sell-stop $17.84 GTC
Commitment = 100 x $25.12 = $2,512
Worst case I get stopped out, 100 x $17.94 = $1,794
I have resigned myself to lose = $728
Total committed till today = $4,090 + $2,512 = $6,602
Willing to lose till today = $6,602 − (300 x $17.94) = ($1,220)

When you broached the subject of the writing of each and every trade details in the journal, Sonia said that she had grown up during a time when writing something down imprinted it in her mind.

"I grew up at a time when writing by hand was the norm. None of the current typing on a laptop business back in the day. It lends a more personal feel to me. I feel more attached to the trade, and it gives me a sense of imprinting the numbers in my mind. I tended to remember things when I wrote them down. Of course, now after the loss of my sight in a car accident I rely on my voice recorder to record my trades using my voice."

It took several weeks before the stock offered a new action Friday. For six weeks straight it kept going up without a reaction. And after six weeks of continuous price rise, the reaction was minimal. Sonia said, "This is the time to go big. Go bigger on your buy now because the stock is saying something to me. It is telling me something is in the offing. We won't know what it is until later, we have to wait until that something actually happens. But now you need to go big."

Chart 7.10

Buy 1500 ALPN at $36.38 Sell-stop $33 GTC
Commitment = 1500 x $36.38 = $54,570
Worst case I get stopped out, 1500 x $33 = $49,500

I have resigned myself to losing = $5,070

Total number of shares = 200 + 100 + 1500 = 1800

Total committed till today = $6,602 + $54,570 = $61,172

Worst case, I will receive = 1800 x $33 = $59,400

Worst case loss = $61,172 - $59,400 = ($1,772)

You notice, amazingly, that even though your total commitment went up, your loss in the worst-case scenario was a smaller percentage of the commitment. You wondered what Sonia knew that you did not.

Five weeks later, the hidden news became public. ALPN was bought by Vertex pharmaceuticals for $64/share. Your 1800 shares were now worth 1800 x $64 = $115,200. Unbelievably, you had doubled your money.

That was the last call you had with Sonia as she had found out that Renata, her usual assistant, had returned from a long holiday in Europe. And Sonia liked Renata's in-person discussions and mark-ins on stock charts. She thanked you for your help.

You opened the chart of ALPN wishing to study it further.

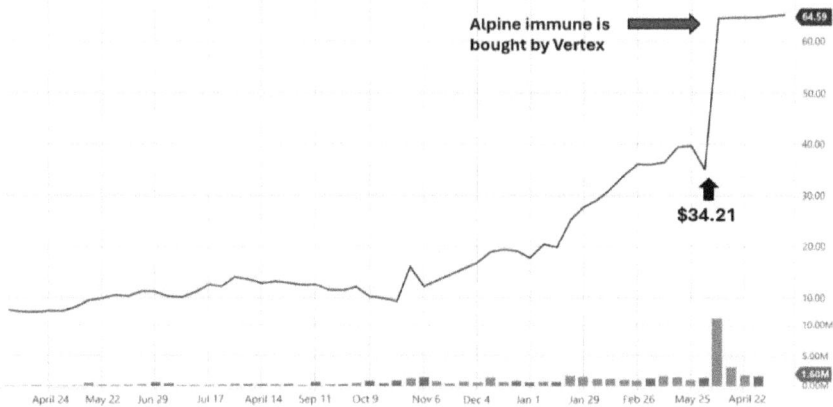

Chart 7.11

The picture told the story. Suddenly, the view came into view. You realized that you too could act as an insider, while being an outsider. It was all there, in the price/volume action. You just had to learn to observe, to interpret and to act. To become the perfect speculator.

.

Test Your Decision-Making Skills
(For The *Serious* Stock Market Student)

The following pages contain a step-by-step chart of a stock you have already read about in this book. To test your skills, imagine you have never seen these charts before. Furthermore, it requires some amount of self-discipline so that you go page by page, chart by chart, without looking at the next page/chart. For each chart, observe, interpret and act. Become the perfect speculator. And place your trade for each chart. A blank page is available for each chart for you to enter your trade with any reasoning behind your decision-making.

Play the game the right way, without paying attention to the score. You will amaze yourself.

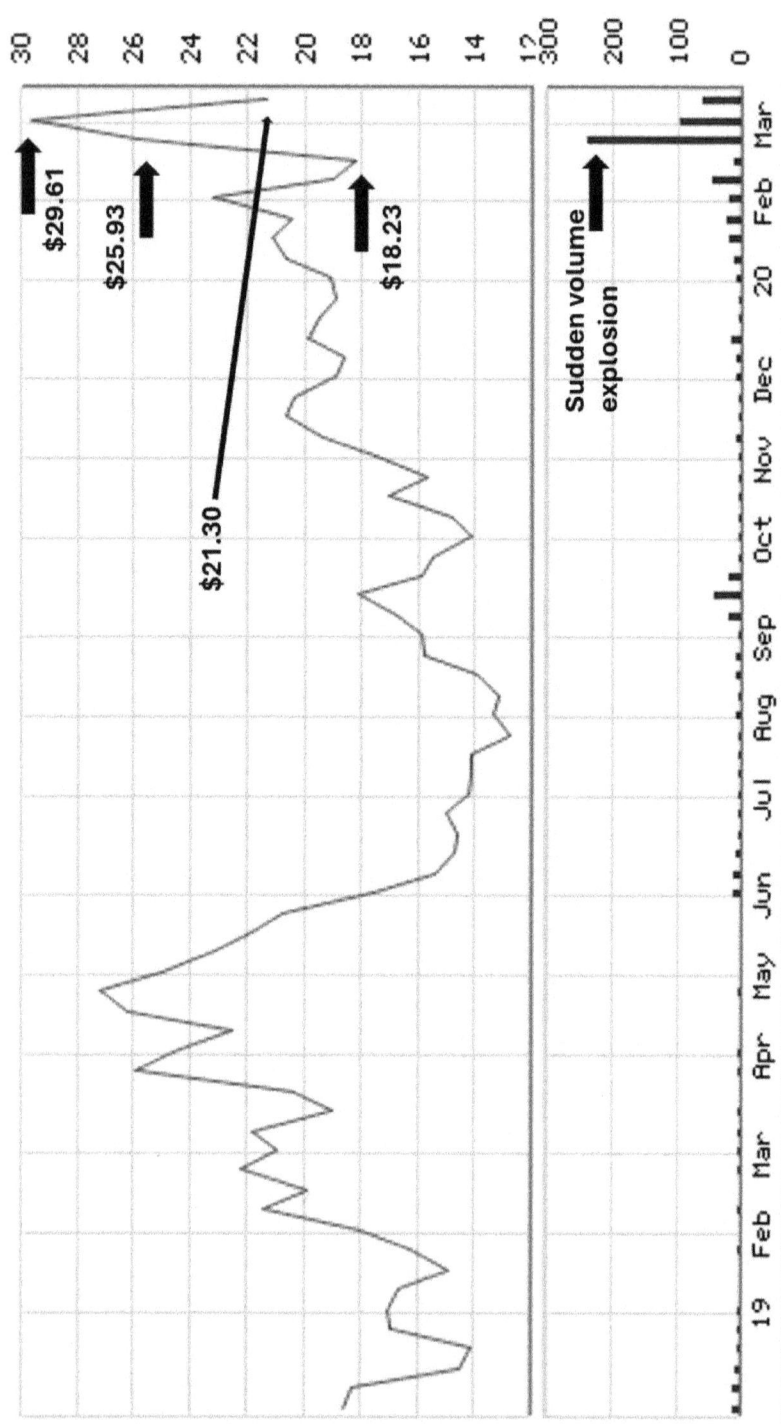

$29.61

$25.93

$21.30

$18.23

Sudden volume
explosion

300
200
100
0

30
28
26
24
22
20
18
16
14
12

19 Feb Mar Apr May Jun Jul Aug Sep Oct Nov Dec 20 Feb Mar

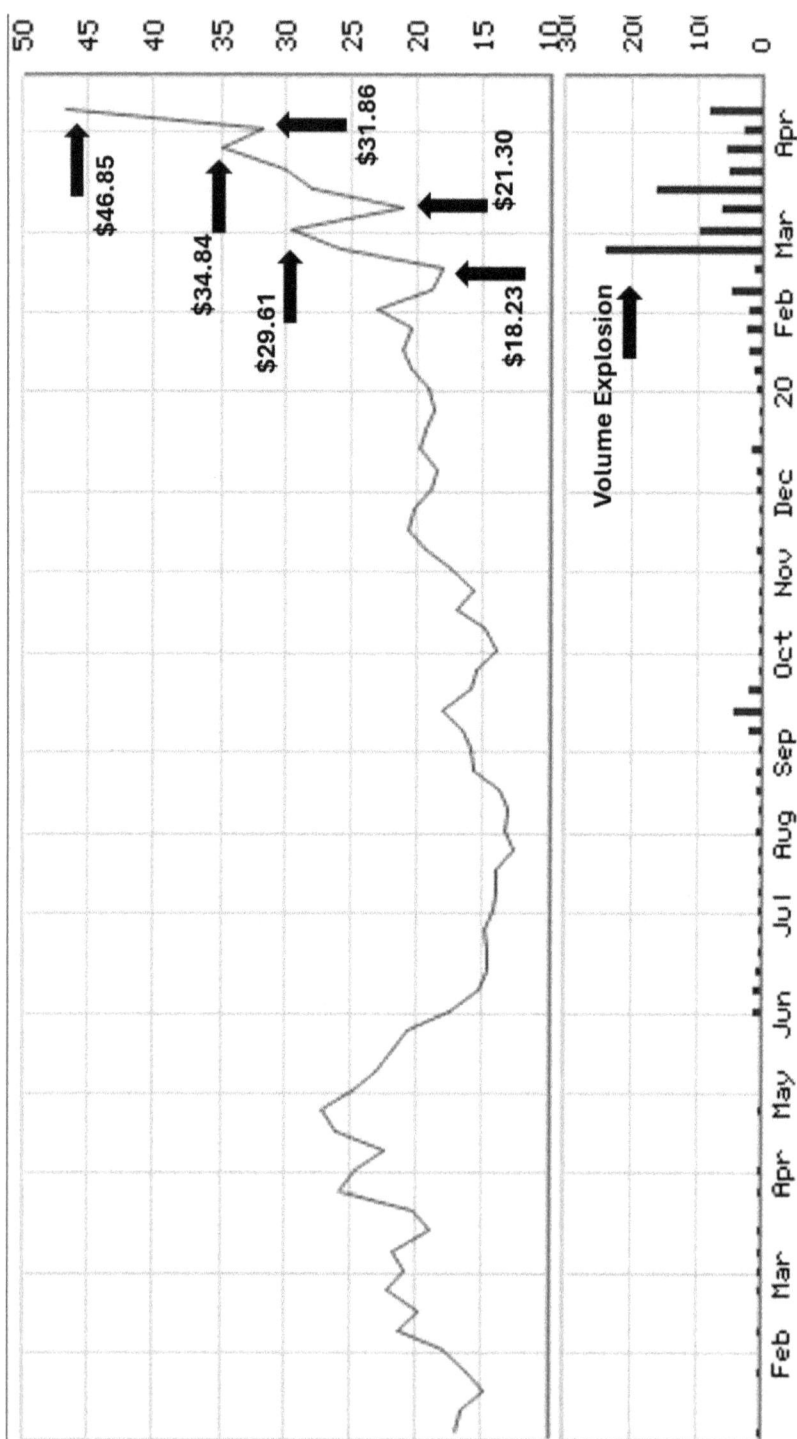

$46.85

$34.84

$29.61

$31.86

$21.30

$18.23

Volume Explosion

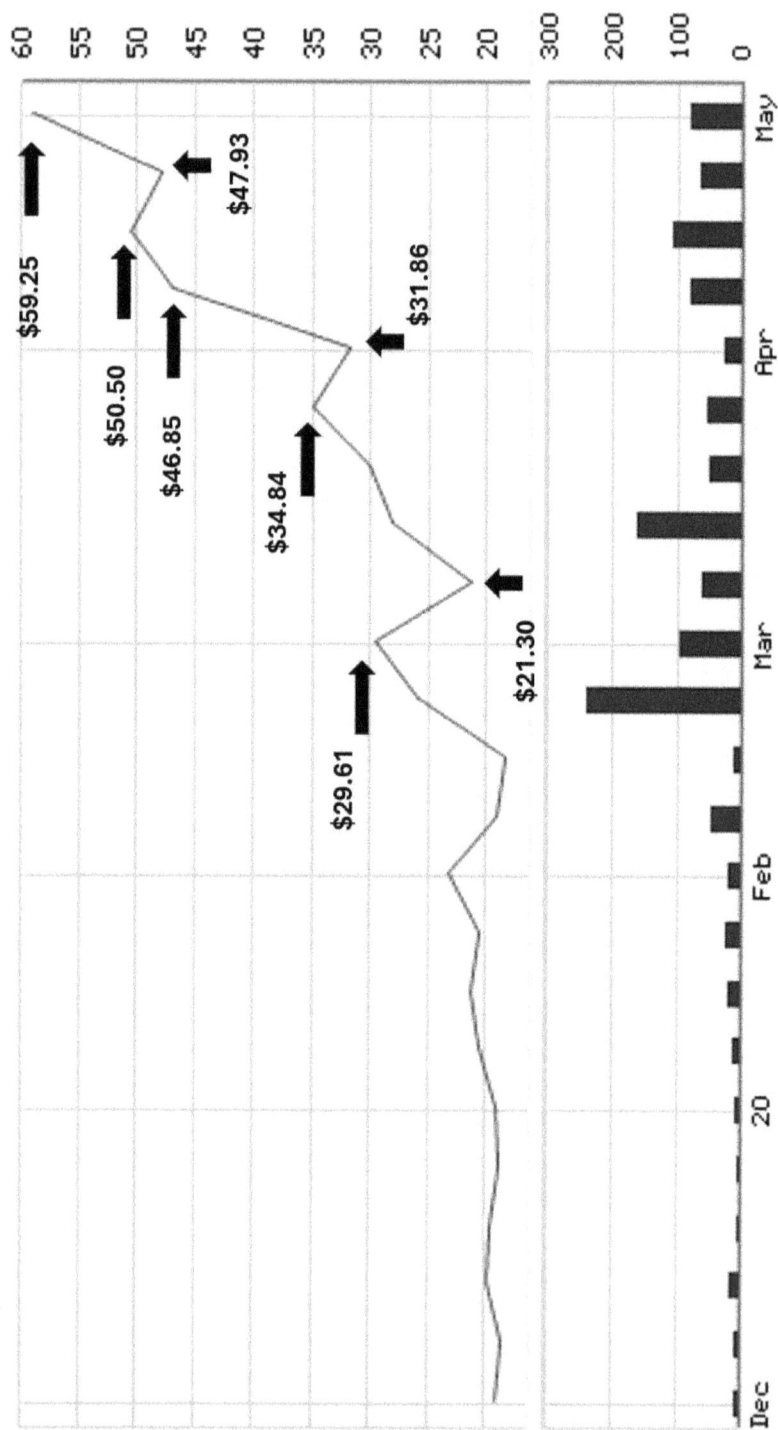

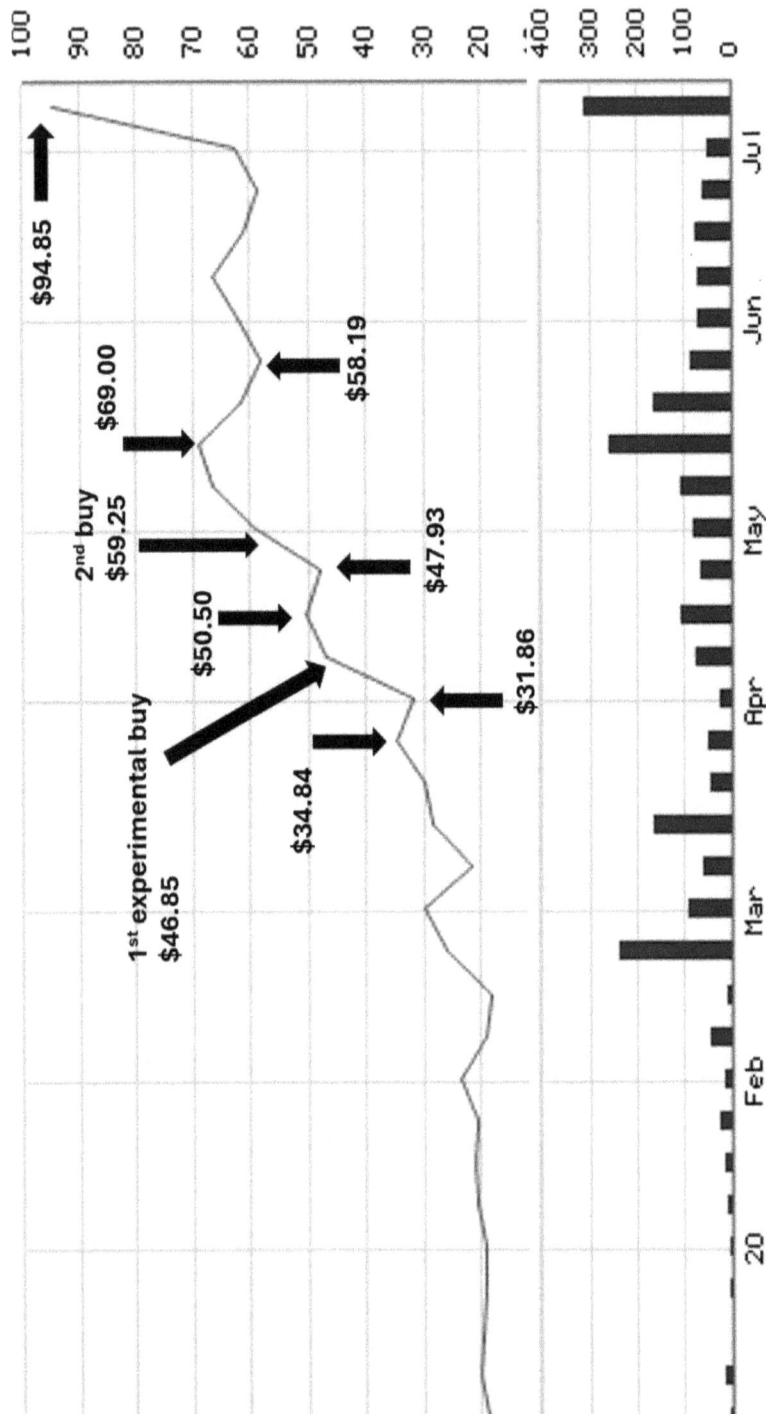

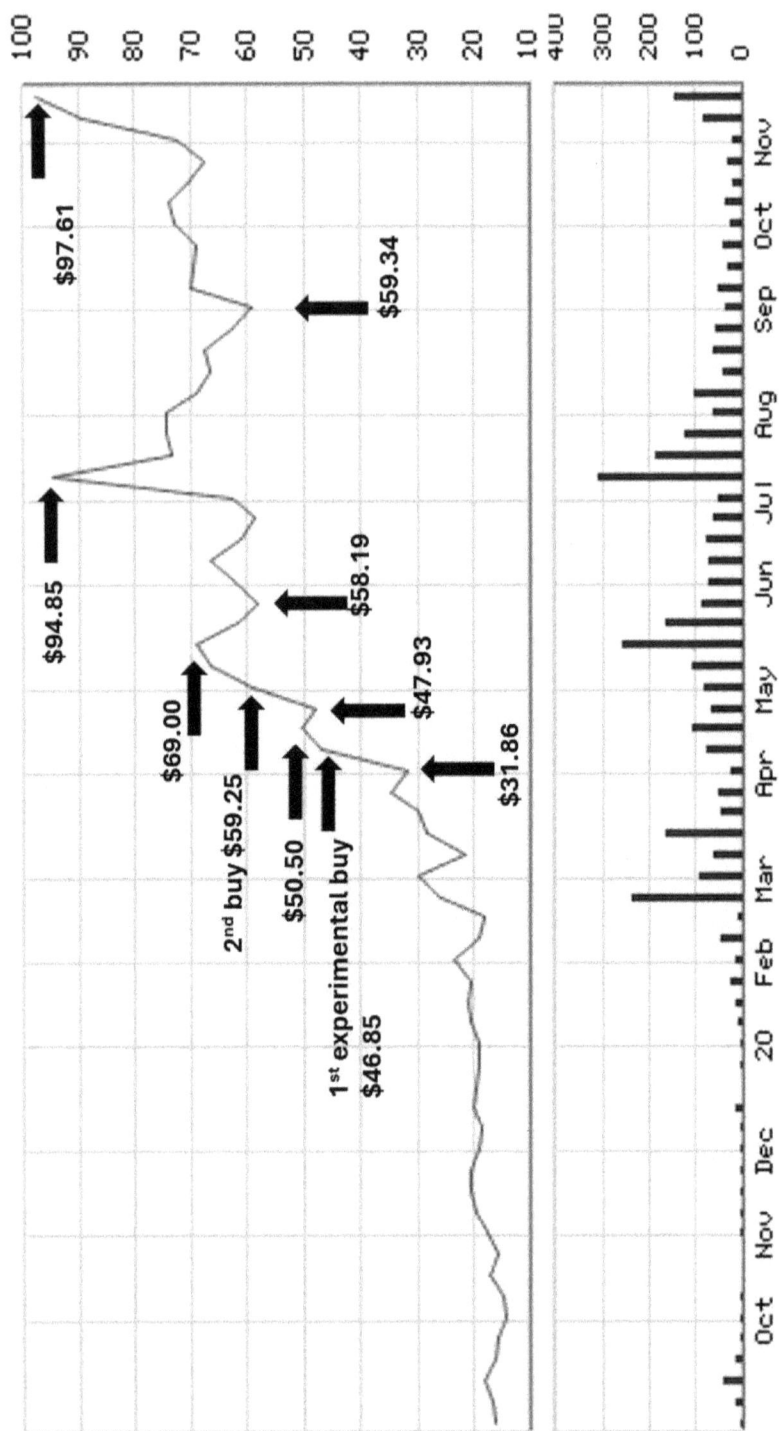

$97.61

$94.85

$59.34

$69.00

$58.19

2nd buy $59.25

$47.93

$50.50

1st experimental buy
$46.85

$31.86

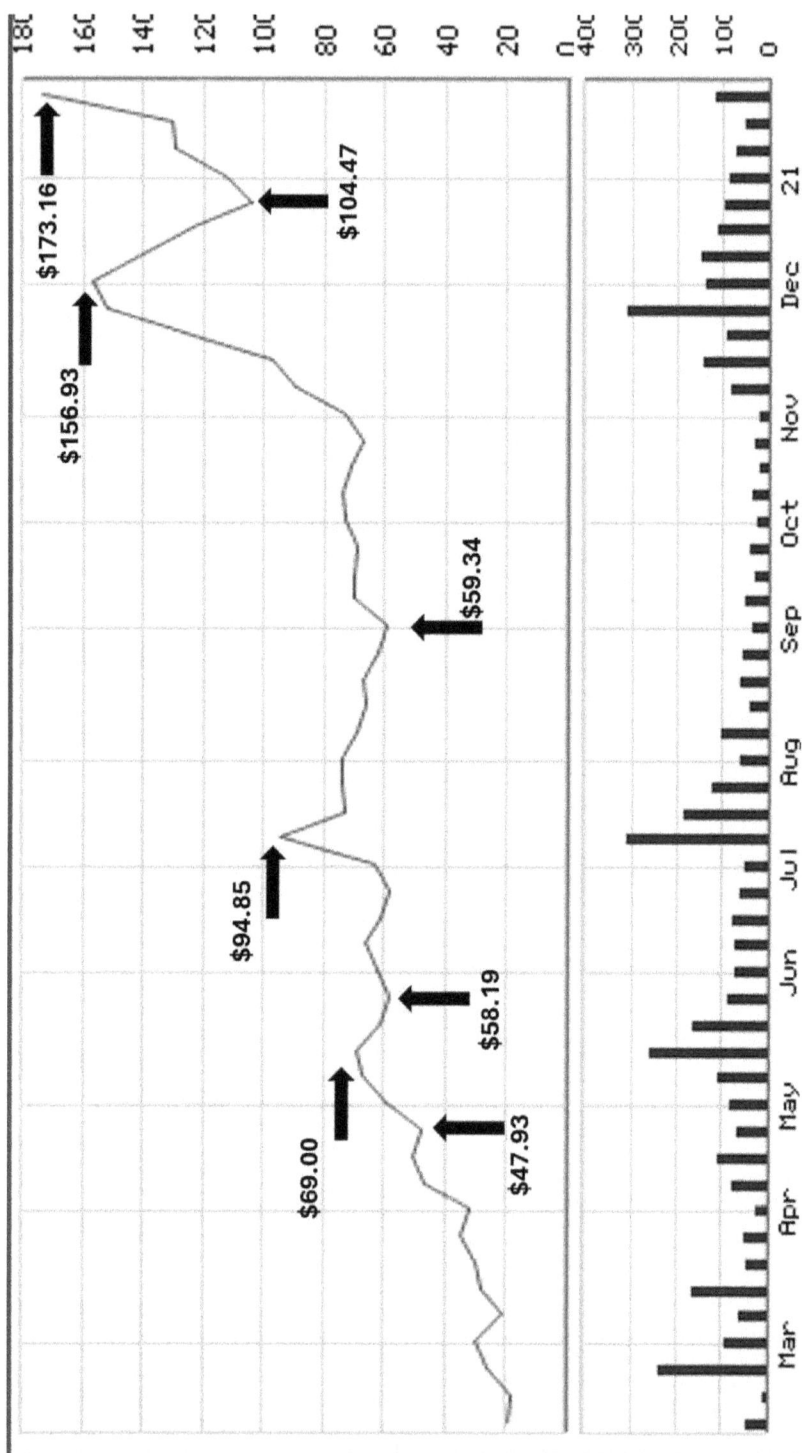

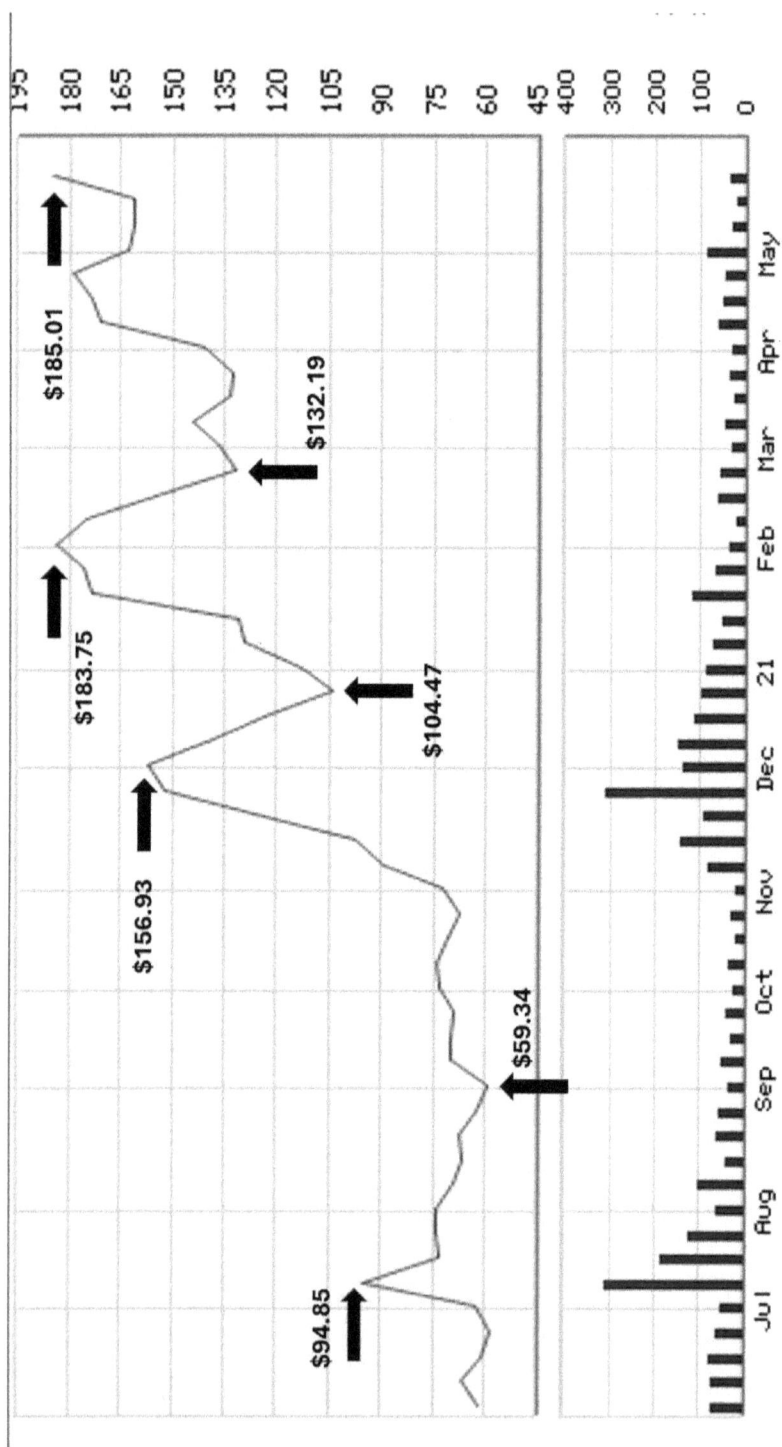

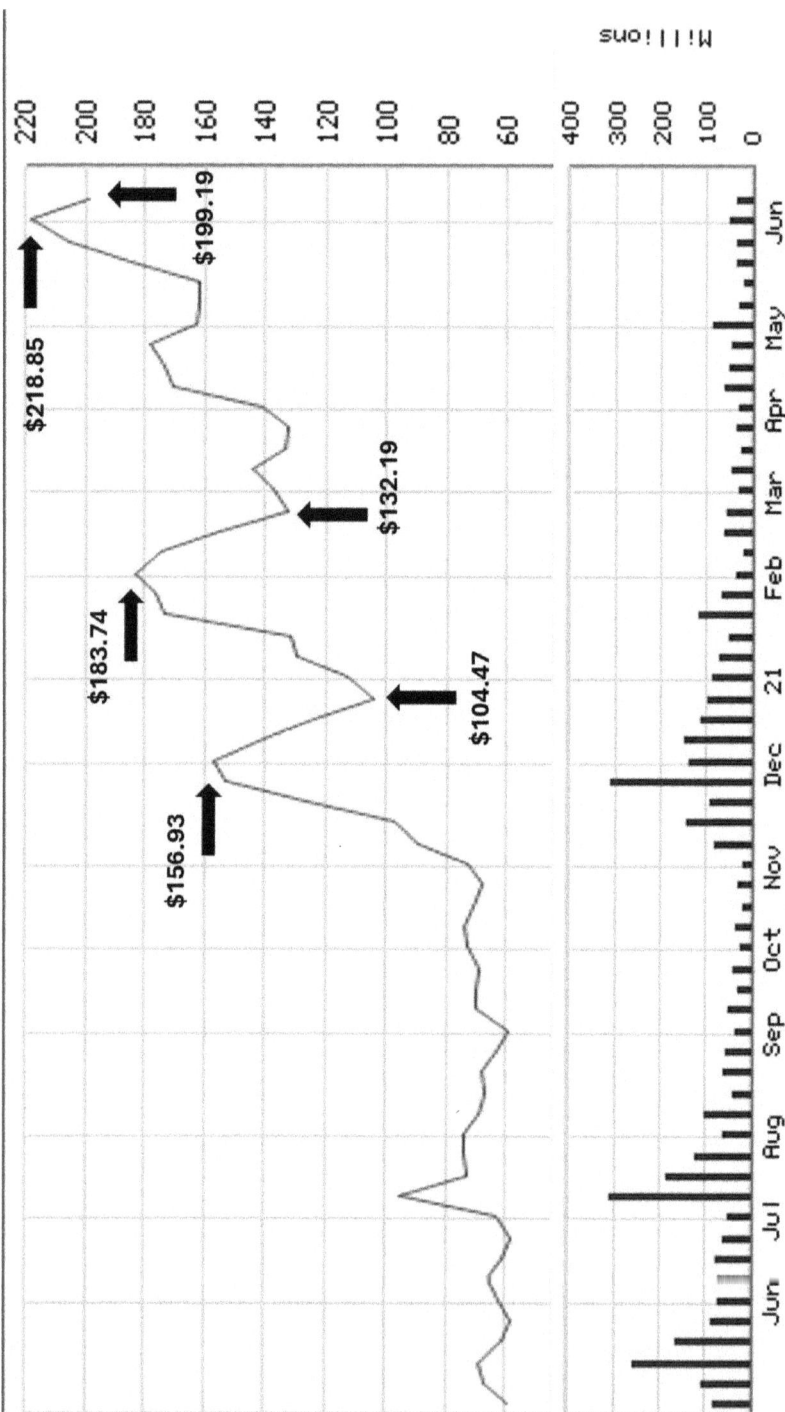

Millions

$218.85

$199.19

$132.19

$183.74

$104.47

$156.93

220
200
180
160
140
120
100
80
60

400
300
200
100
0

Jun May Apr Mar Feb 21 Dec Nov Oct Sep Aug Jul Jun

204

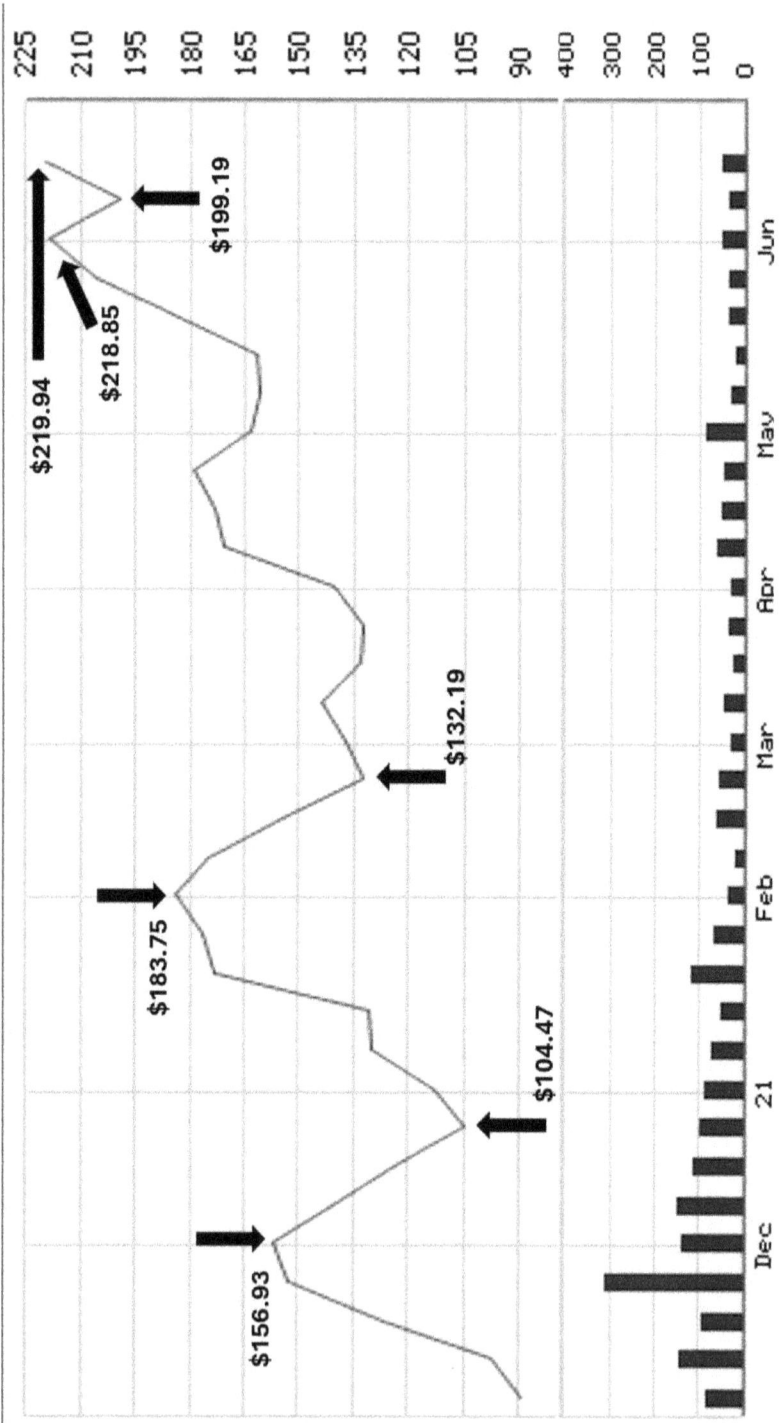

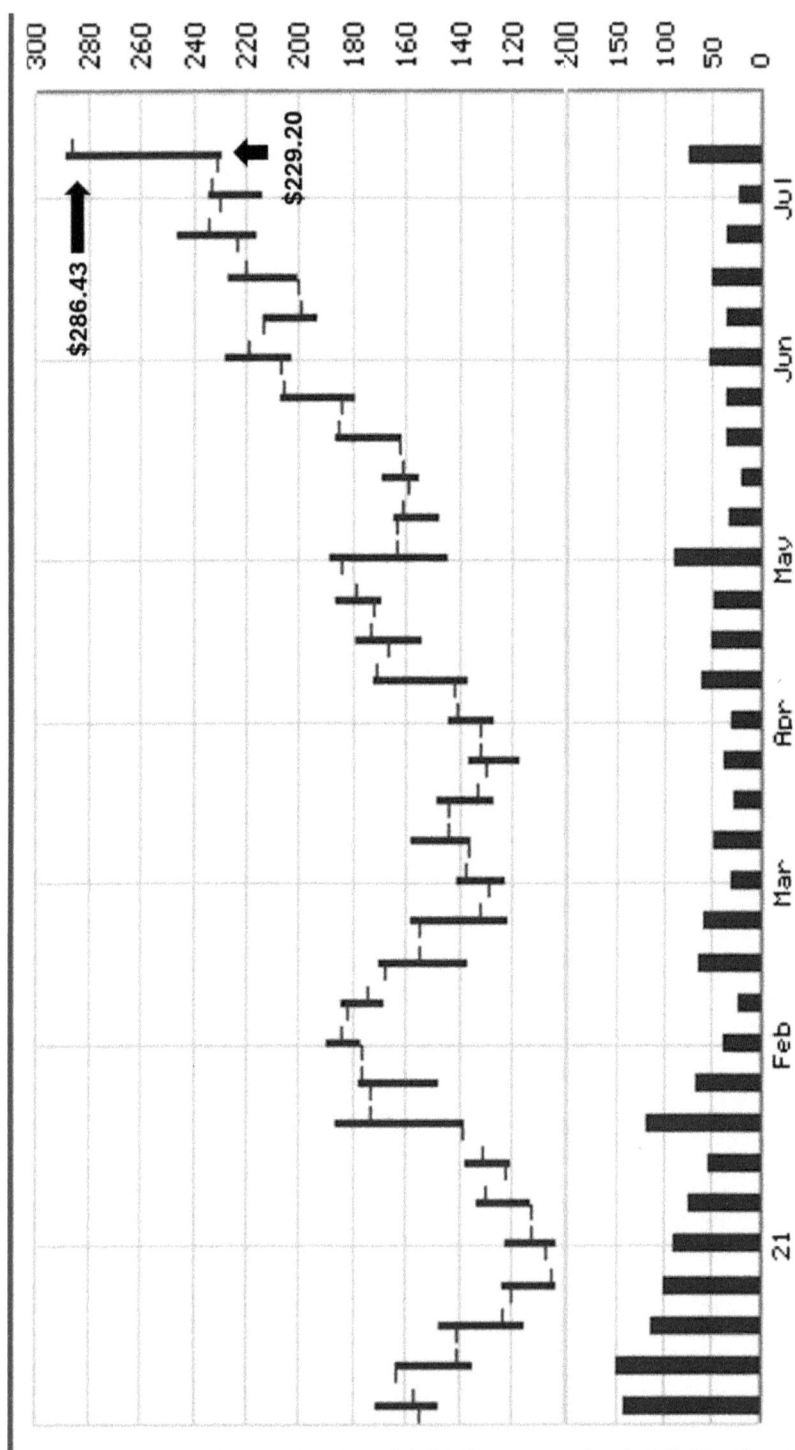

$286.43

$229.20

208

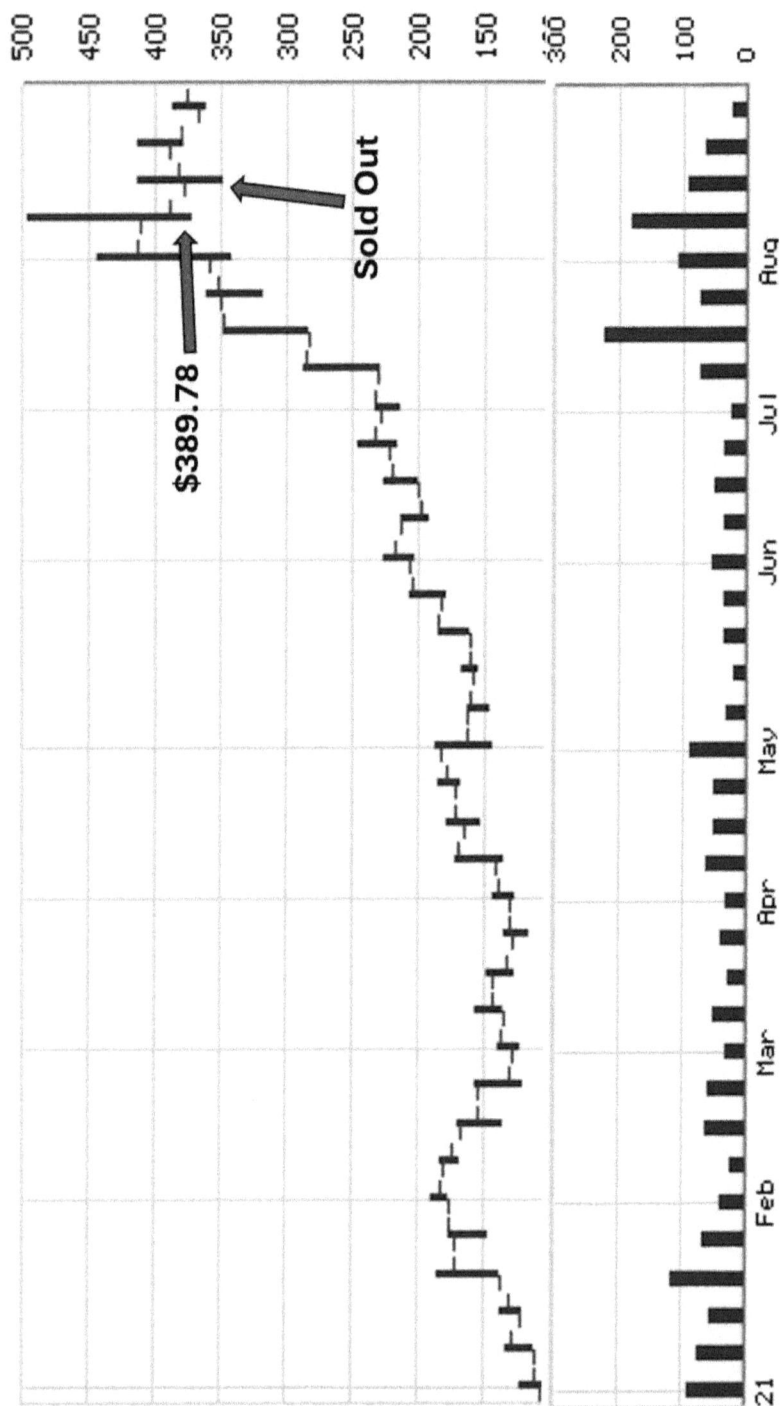

Now, You Are On Your Way
To Become The Perfect Speculator
(You just need experience of at least
one full up cycle and one full down cycle)

Other Works From The Author

About The Author:

BradKoteshwar.com

More From The Author:

The Perfect Stock: How a 7000% move was set-up, started and finished in
an astonishing 52 weeks
(Also available in Hindi version)

The Perfect Speculator: How To Win Big In Up Markets And Lose
Nothing In Down Markets
(Also available in Spanish, German, Hindi and Chinese versions)

The Perfect Fool: Foolish Lessons From The Best Stocks Of 2021
The Perfect Watchlist – 1
The Perfect Chart
The Perfect Fool – Volume 2

For The More <u>Serious</u> Stock Market Student:

ThePerfectSpeculator.com
A unique 10-week stock market course (*a course like no other*)

www.ingramcontent.com/pod-product-compliance
Lightning Source LLC
Chambersburg PA
CBHW042124190326
41521CB00017B/2597